D1071571

fragments

MARILYN MONROE

fragments

poems, intimate notes, letters

EDITED BY

STANLEY BUCHTHAL

AND

BERNARD COMMENT

FARRAR, STRAUS AND GIROUX

NEW YORK

Farrar, Straus and Giroux
18 West 18th Street, New York 10011

Printed in the United States of America
First edition, 2010

Photograph credits can be found on page 239.

Library of Congress Control Number: 2010932487
ISBN: 978-0-374-15835-4

Designed by Valérie Gautier

www.fsgbooks.com

10 9 8 7 6 5 4 3 2 1

CONTENTS

Editors' note vii

Personal note (1943) 5
Undated poems 15
"Record" black notebook (around 1951) 33
Other "Record" notebook (around 1955) 51
Waldorf-Astoria stationery (1955) 69
Italian agenda (1955 or 1956) 89
Parkside House stationery (1956) 105
Roxbury notes (1958) 125
Red livewire notebook (1958) 135
Fragments and notes 149
Kitchen notes (1955 or 1956) 175
Lee and Paula Strasberg 185
Letter to Dr. Hohenberg (1956) 201
Letter to Dr. Greenson (1961) 205
Written answers to an interview (1962) 217

SUPPLEMENTS
Some books from Marilyn Monroe's personal library *226*
The favorite photo *228*
Funeral eulogy by Lee Strasberg *231*
Chronology *232*
Literary constellation *234*
Acknowledgments *237*

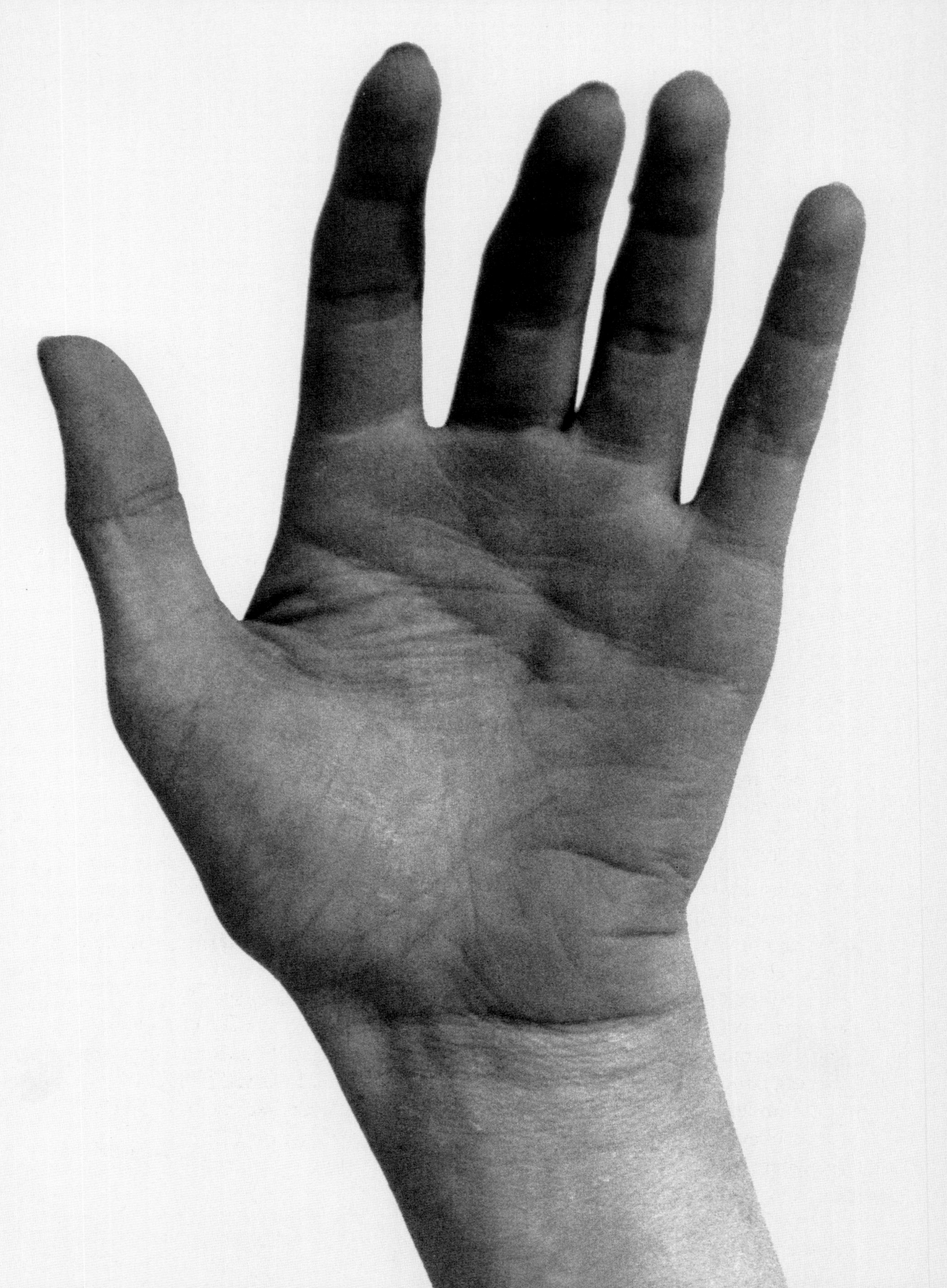

EDITORS' NOTE

Norma Jeane Mortenson was born under the sign of Gemini, and she described herself as having two natures: "Jekyll and Hyde, two in one." Even the initials of her stage name (which, according to one story, were suggested to her by the clearly visible "M"s formed by the lines of her palms) supported this duality, as did the pseudonym, Zelda Zonk, that she used while escaping incognito from Hollywood to New York.

In her lifetime, under pressure from the studios, the media created a joyful and radiant image of Marilyn Monroe, even to the point of making her out to be a "dumb blonde." One remembers her parts in *Gentlemen Prefer Blondes, The Seven Year Itch*, *How to Marry a Millionaire*, and *Let's Make Love*. Anything contrary to this artificial image was not welcome. There was no room for a melancholic Marilyn. The icon was not allowed to have an opposite side.

Yet, like a medal, she did have two sides. The sunny and luminous one of the sparkling blonde, and the darker one of the excessive perfectionist who sought absolutes and for whom life (work, friendships, and love affairs) could only lead to disappointment. "I think I have a gay side in me and also a sad side," Marilyn confided in an interview.

Her friend Marlon Brando expressed perfectly the shock people felt when her death was announced: "Everybody stopped work, and you could see all that day the same expressions on their faces, the same thought: 'How can a girl with success, fame, youth, money, beauty . . . how could she kill herself?' Nobody could understand it because those are the things that everybody wants, and they can't believe that life wasn't important to Marilyn Monroe, or that her life was elsewhere."

Marilyn's hand, 1946

There are thousands of photographs of this icon. Her image has been used in many, sometimes brutal, ways. But in this book a new world of truthfulness and overwhelming clarity is being thrown open. A hitherto unknown and unseen Marilyn is revealed.

On her death in 1962, Marilyn Monroe's personal possessions were bequeathed to Lee Strasberg, and when he in turn died in 1982, his young widow, Anna Strasberg, inherited this large and uncataloged collection, which included dresses, cosmetics, pictures, books, receipts, and so forth. Many years later, while sorting out Lee Strasberg's papers, she found two boxes of poems and other manuscripts written by Marilyn. Not knowing what to do with these, she asked a family friend, Stanley Buchthal, for advice. Some months later, at an art collectors' dinner, Stanley told Bernard Comment, a French essayist and editor, about Anna Strasberg's find in order to get his opinion of the unpublished materials. That was the start of the adventure that became this book.

As far as has been possible to determine, the texts are placed in chronological order. Words printed in red are the editors' and correct spelling mistakes, add missing words, or suggest possible readings of indecipherable words. The ordering of fragments of very disparate documents has been an attempt at reconstruction and hence at interpretation. The flow of Marilyn's thoughts on individual pages, and from one successive page to another, is indicated by red arrows (black arrows are Marilyn's own).

It is possible that other texts written by Marilyn will surface in the years or decades to come. For the moment, this book contains every available text, excepting her technical notes on acting. In any case, these writings reveal a young woman who was dissatisfied with issues of surface appearance and who was seeking the truth at the heart of both things and people.

Only lovers of clichés will be surprised that the Hollywood actress was passionately fond of literature, although this fact cannot be illustrated merely by the pictures collected in this book. (Still: how many actresses from that period do we know who sometimes took pains to be photographed reading or holding a book?) In a 1960 interview with the French journalist Georges Belmont, Marilyn recalled the beginning of her career: "Nobody could imagine what I did when I wasn't shooting, because they didn't see me at previews or premieres or parties. It's simple: I was going to school! I'd never finished high school, so I started going to UCLA at night, because during the day I had small parts in pictures. I took courses in the history of literature and the history of this country, and I started to read a lot, stories by wonderful writers." Her library contained four hundred books, ranging from such classics as Milton, Dostoyevsky, and Whitman to contemporary writers, including Hemingway, Beckett, and Kerouac.

Arthur Miller played a part in her development as a reader, too, recommending Carl Sandburg's six-volume biography of Abraham Lincoln, which she devoured. But some years before they were involved, Marilyn had already tackled James Joyce's *Ulysses*.

As we know, Marilyn inspired numerous painters: Dalí, De Kooning, and Warhol, among others. She also felt a real interest in painting—in the painters of the Italian Renaissance, such as Botticelli; Goya, especially his demons ("I know this man very well, we have the same dreams, I have had the same dreams since I was a child"); Degas, whose ballet dancer she gazed at in wonder when taken to see a private collection; and also Rodin, whose *Hand of God* she admired at length in the Metropolitan Museum of Art.

From all these examples emerges a cultured and curious Marilyn who had a strong desire to understand others, the outside world, destiny, and, of course, herself. She took notes, swiftly setting down her feelings and thoughts and expressing her wonder. Some may be surprised at her spelling mistakes, in which, most probably, a form of dyslexia is detectable. But readers of Marcel Proust's correspondence (Marilyn read *Swann's Way* on the set of *Love Nest* in 1951) will have seen worse. The very Proust who, answering the question "to which failings are you most lenient?" replied unhesitatingly, "spelling mistakes," and who, in one of his letters, wrote this strange and beautiful phrase: "Each spelling mistake is the expression of a desire."

The collection of documents revealed here is nothing less than a treasure trove. We owe its appearance to Anna Strasberg and her sons, Adam and David, who, during the preparation of this book, have embraced the opportunity to uncover a hitherto undervalued, even unknown dimension of Marilyn's personality. From beginning to end we have shared their desire to create a book that, we would like to think, would have pleased its author. Marilyn once confessed to a journalist: "I think Lee probably changed my life more than any other human being. That's why I love to go to the Actors Studio whenever I'm in New York." Perhaps Strasberg, more than other people, had sensed who Marilyn really was.

One of the remarkable insights these documents offer is the sense that

Marilyn was, until the end, planning for the future. Among other projects, she hoped over time to play the great Shakespearean roles, from Juliet to Lady Macbeth. She also pursued her idea of creating a new production company in association with Marlon Brando.

Some texts will give rise to interpretation and comment. But there is nothing dirty or low, no gossip in this book; that was not Marilyn's way. What the notes reveal is intimacy without showiness, the seismic measuring of a soul. They take nothing away from Marilyn's mystery but rather make the mystery more material. She was an elusive star with a magnetic force that sent compasses haywire whenever she got close.

To this day, her face, her eyes, her lips appear all around the world. Innumerable actors and pop singers take her as a reference, a definitive model: to sound like her, to act like her, in advertisements and music videos and films. Songs are composed for her—among them this famous one, by Elton John and Bernie Taupin: "Goodbye Norma Jeane (. . .) / Loneliness was tough / The toughest role you ever played / Hollywood created a superstar / And pain was the price you paid / Even when you died / Oh the press still hounded you / All the papers had to say / Was that Marilyn was found in the nude."

This book does not attempt to show her stripped bare but, rather, simply as she was. Through these poems and written papers, she's more alive than ever.

Stanley Buchthal
Bernard Comment

fragments

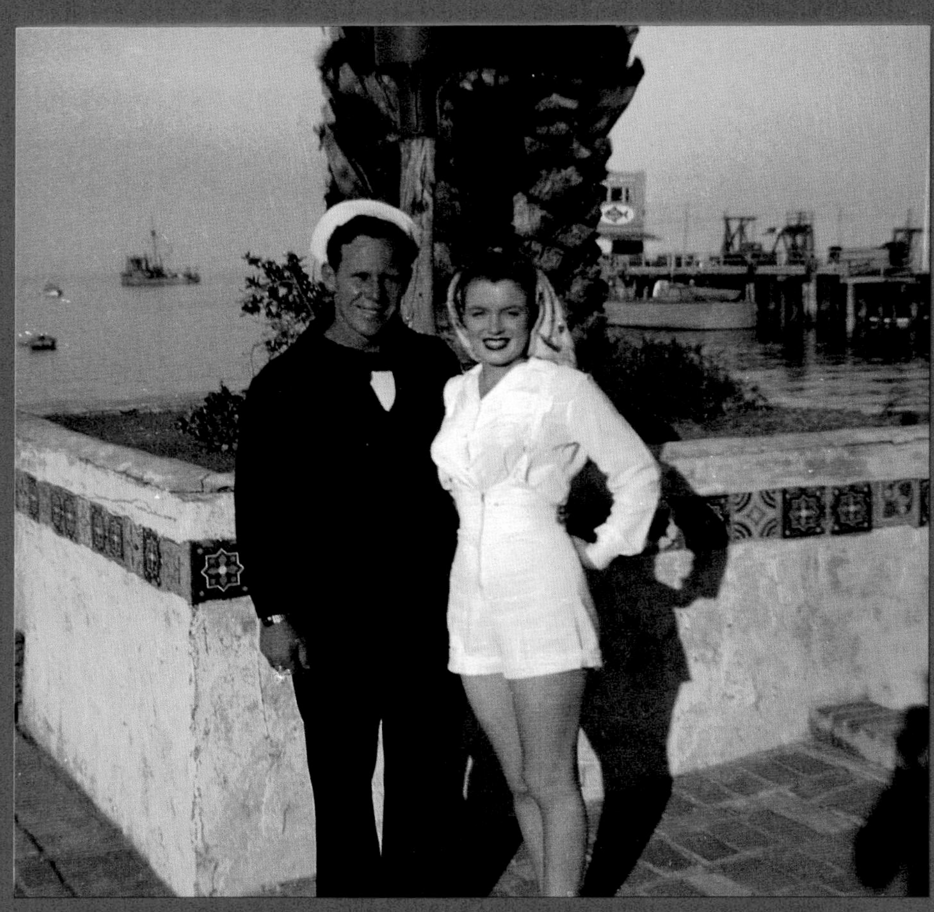

Jim Dougherty and Norma Jeane, Catalina Island, fall of 1943

PERSONAL NOTE

1943

Norma Jeane married James Dougherty when she turned sixteen, the age of consent in California, on June 19, 1942, thereby escaping the threat of being returned to an orphanage when her foster family moved out of state. Dougherty was born in April 1921 and was five years older than she was. At the end of 1943, the young couple settled for a few months on Catalina Island off the coast of Los Angeles, a fashionable resort before the war. It is likely that this long note, uncharacteristically typed, was written at this time.

One can't help being surprised, even impressed, by the maturity of this seventeen-year-old girl, whose feelings of disillusionment are plain from the first sentence, as she examines her marriage and what she expects from life, and faces the fear of her husband's betrayal. Nevertheless, the disjointedness of the text reveals turbulent emotions.

The "other woman" she mentions might be a reference to Doris Ingram, her young husband's former girlfriend and a Santa Barbara beauty queen.

The couple were divorced on September 13, 1946.

my relationship with him was basically insecure from the first night I spent alone with him. He was very insecure not perhaps so much of himself but of how I a girl 6 yr younger would react - actually in the beginning I would never have stayed with him but for his love of classical music his intellect which made a pretense at being more then it was and his desire to bring out any maturer qualities envolving personality or secual relations with me. It was a period in which I ran up against many doubts as to whether this young man of 21 was in unreality my surpressed edea of a dream man - probaleling I was greatly attracted to him as one of the ~~only~~ few young men I had no sexual repulsion for besides which it gave me a false sense of security to feel that he was endowed with more over-welming qualities which I did not possess ——— on paper it all begins to sound terribly logical but the secret mid-night meetings the fugetive glance stolen in others company the sharing of the ocean, moon & stars and air aloneness made it a ~~to~~ romantic adventure ~~for~~ which a young, rather shy girl who didnt always give that impression because of her desire to belong & develope can thrive on -- I had always felt a need to live up to that expectation of my elders having been not ~~a per~~ in a precosious manner an unusually mature child for my age - and at ~~twel~~ 10, 11, 12 & 13 when my closer companions were all persons of 4 to 6 yrs - advancement this envirement of peo. into which I at first inadvertantly fell made all the problems of adolesance, that painful inbetween age, where one yearns only to be accepted in <u>ones</u> <u>own</u> age group, more intensified, so that at 15, I felt strongly the pattern of insecurity I had developed -- only ~~we~~ with people younger or older was I confortable and in such presences I became an advanced child who fitted in easily except on grounds where her own

- continued -

age group of 15-21) was involved probably my frustrations are no greater then those of any teenage girl but some overcome it by loosing principle & intelligence to a degree where I felt that eventually this would combat not conquer for them. All my unfounded jealousies were surpressed by my desire to find myself a full person ready to face less superficial problems then the typical teenager is supposed to have.

I was a very small delicatly built girl - at 15 I had done a play T.V. - show a leading part modeling occasionally with innumerable opportunities movies to contracts - steady modeling so that to an outsider it might not be concievable that I had taken my small insecurities and built them up into a nervous tension which although it had outlets was always present ~~whi~~ with so some people no apparent reason. ~~during most of my~~ during the ~~summer ther~~ year there would be days or weeks when I wanted only to have occasional company when desired - to busy myself in reading so that any attempt at ajustment to a situation which looked slightly forboding became an exausting process -- I was an intense introvert probably but because I loved people and had friends wherevere I cared to cultivate them it was perhaps balanced more then it might be -- if I had not any agreeable or charming social patterns the unfortunate thing~~s~~ was that any/or coldness withdrawing was deliberate and that although I recognized this feeling I had no desire except in very passionate moods to overcome my feelings -- very few people except my more sensitive acuaintences sensed this and accepted it fully he did not - for being in himself a person who had in different envirement my problems to a lesser degree.

3

One experiance which I have not analized objectively nor will I probably be able to occured one evening - the past night we had spent together my being in a bitchy withdrawn mood the evening was rather weary and weighted with almost a distrust of him & his relation to this other girl which I at first would only aproach (and not to accept in a very roundabout manner so that we parted rather cooly and abruptly making no plans to meet ~~secretly~~ the next night, I being the romantic esthetic1 soul I am believed that like some great lover he would know I was waiting for him unfortunaly he did not appear and I began to berate him & myself - myself for being unrealistic ~~n~~ mean undomonstretive and for allowing myself to care in a situation I felt I had been drawn into and then forced to grow with first by he then by my consious being slowly falling into the habits which my actions set -

I think that only a person who remembers growing up might very clearly & completely see what an objective analitical view I an trying to establish suceeding in becoming a trifle to pompass about my own reletively simple thoughts but then its very difficult for me to set down on paper as if talking to a second person those bare truths & emotions I felt - perhaps even poetic but which if I wrote them in thier naturl form I fear I might disgard right into the wastepaper basket -

note) listening to the little girl crying in the hall it seems that at times children have remarkable perseption & ~~insite~~ insight and in some even a very humane trait which while in the prosess of growing up one loses touch with - (oh damn! I get so carried away that I completely sidetrack myself good intentions or no) anyway finding myself ofhandedly stood up snubbed my first feeling was not of anger - but the numb pain of rejection & hurt at the { destruction ~~of~~ / lose of some sort of edealistic image of true love.

My first impulse then was one of complete subjection humiliation, alonement to the male counterpart. (all this thought & writting has made my hands tremble but I just want to keep pouring it out until that great pot in the mind is, though not emptied, ~~relieves~~ relieved - I know when I sit down & read this I will blanche at the thought of having written so much crap - (you see side-tracked again) - then - out of sheer desparation I sopose I stood & waiting for one hour & a quarter suffering as greatly ~~&~~ though not as ~~notel~~ notebly or sobbing as Duses & crying not hystericaly ~~but~~ just large drops ~~fal~~ trickling down my nose making me scratch my face - underneath I was worried that he might come & see me in that piteful state eyes red-nose shinning hair falling stragling curtaining one eye <u>end of</u> evening.

Then came the 2nd act while speaking - rather she spoke (one of those I had been avoiding I discovered & that he had spent the evening & most of the morning hours with the <u>other woman</u> to be prosaic & I thanked God I had waylaid him on the beach to protest my undying love - rejection I could endure but making a fool of myself even if he had been sincere in his love ~~I could~~ my pride could not take - also the fact that I was so foolishly loyal and that I did not have a chance to wound him in some childish fashion was another blow to my as yet unsteady ego - I now would like a chance at a third act - the unsuspecting male and ~~then~~ the vengful female, ~~el~~ but now I'm only fooling myself if I do get my last act I will portray the heroine who bravely suffers tucking it all away to use as barage ~~form~~ some now unknown man.

(this is all making me feel easier and perhaps spending the night alone will not be a trial such as the one I forced myself through last night - I would like to see him though as I'm leaving this place tomorrow - why isn't anything plain & commonplace ordinary & easy -

I guess I'm to emotional in the wrong spots -

but if things weren't like that I would probably bore myself - although if I were different I would hardly know the defference (I've been smoking and it is a filthy habit (it's not one of mine yet) I have the most unpleasant smell and ~~tel~~ taste in my mouth as if I ~~were~~ had chewed raw tobacco over a sustained amount of time.

Why is it that after all this sensible talk the thought of meeting him still not uncovering my feelings makes my pulse beat and I feel the blood flush my body (if I had any sense disipline or courage I would not even look for the boy who won't be there yet I know know that at 12 o clock I will feel another surge of resentment).

I think my love if you must call it that was mostly that wonderful titulaling feeling of of being wanted, loved & cared for ~~by-e~~ & any sexual ~~attech~~ attraction.

~~I-thing~~ I think perhaps I would be freer tonight & might even be able to say I love you looking into his eyes straight & feeling a tinge of hate or something akin to it.

to show its my feminine being that wants satisfaction last night I was so badly sunburnt that I wore only a sweater & no bra - it gave me a sensual feeling I thought he ~~my~~ might share - now there is the question of whether he lied to me - if he loved us both I could accept that but if he lied when he said I was first & foremost and that if this relationship ever differed he would share this information with me for as he himself said, I would not want to play second fiddle.

There is one span of time in which I knew he was honest but then she had not ~~met~~ entered our lives - (as you see I am still quite an optomist and soon I hope I can laugh about this - a laughter without that protective false ring.

Its hard not to try and rationalize and protect your own feelings but eventually that makes the acceptance of truth more difficult -

And I was planning to come here for two weeks - if I do the play I can go through 2 weeks of hell but if not I either have to make a very fast adjustment or find another vacation spot.

For someone like me its wrong to go through ~~threw~~ thorough self analisis - I do it enough in thought generalities enough.

Its not to much fun to know yourself to well or think you do - everyone needs a little conciet to carry them ~~past-the~~ through & past the falls

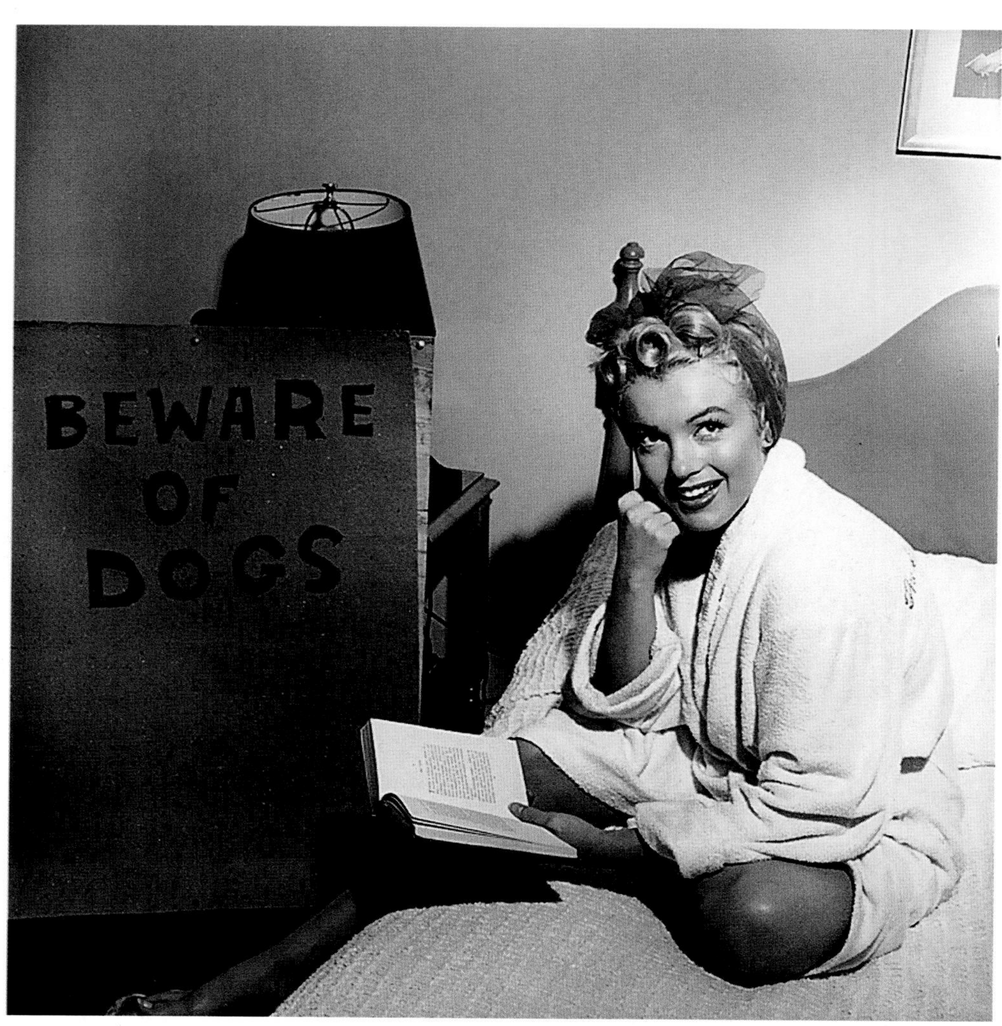

Marilyn during the filming of *Niagara*, 1952
Marilyn reading Heinrich Heine

UNDATED POEMS

Marilyn Monroe wrote poemlike texts or fragments on loose-leaf paper and in notebooks. She showed her work only to intimate friends, in particular to Norman Rosten, a college friend of Arthur Miller with whom she became very close. A Brooklyn-based novelist, he encouraged Marilyn to continue writing. In the book he wrote about her (*Marilyn Among Friends*), he concluded, "She had the instinct and reflexes of the poet, but she lacked the control."

It is likely that the poetic form, or more generally the fragment, allowed her to express short, lightning bursts of feeling—but who could hear that frail voice, the very opposite of the radiant star? Arthur Miller wrote strikingly: "To have survived, she would have had to be either more cynical or even further from reality than she was. Instead, she was a poet on a street corner trying to recite to a crowd pulling at her clothes."

Life, —

I am of both of your directions

~~Life~~ —

Some how remaining ~~downward~~ changing
the most

But strong as a cobweb in the
wind — I exist more with the ~~cold~~ glistening frost —
but my beaded rays have the colors I've
seen in a painting — ah life they
have cheated you

Life—
I am of both of your directions
~~Life~~
Somehow remaining hanging downward
the most
but strong as a cobweb in the
wind—I exist more with the cold glistening frost.
But my beaded rays have the colors I've
seen in a painting~~s~~—ah life they
have cheated you

Note: Marilyn apparently wrote several variations on the theme of the twofold course of life ("life in both directions") and the delicate, sometimes invisible "cobweb," revealed by dew and resistant to wind—in particular a poem entitled "To the Weeping Willow" that was published in Norman Rosten's book about Marilyn: "I stood beneath your limbs / And you flowered and finally / clung to me, / and when the wind struck with the earth / and sand—you clung to me. / Thinner than a cobweb I, / sheerer than any— / but it did attach itself / and held fast in strong winds / life—of which at singular times / I am both of your directions— / somehow I remain hanging downward the most, / as both of your directions pull me."

Oh damn I wish that I were
dead — absolutly nonexistent —
gone away from here — from
everywhere but how would I ~~do it~~
There is always bridges — the Brooklyn
Bridge — ~~no not the Brooklyn Bridge~~
~~because~~ But I love that Bridge (everything is beautiful from there & the air is so clean) walking it seems
peaceful ~~there~~ even with all those
cars going crazy underneathe — So
it would have to be some other bridge
an ugly one and with no view — except
I ~~particularly~~ like in particular all bridges — theres some-
-thing about them and besides ~~there~~ I've
never seen an ugly bridge

Oh damn I wish that I were
dead—absolutely nonexistent—
gone away from here—from
everywhere but how would I ~~do it~~
There is always bridges—the Brooklyn
bridge~~— no not the Brooklyn Bridge~~
~~because~~ But I love that bridge (everything is beautiful from there
and the air is so clean) walking it seems
peaceful ~~there~~ even with all those
cars going crazy underneath. So
it would have to be some other bridge
an ugly one and with no view—except
I ~~particularly~~ like in particular all bridges—there's something about them and besides ~~these~~ I've
never seen an ugly bridge

stones on the walk
every color There is
I stare down at you
like there a hirizon—
the space air is between us beckoning bekoning
and foam many stories up besides—
my feet frieghtened
as my grasp towards you

Stones on the walk
every color there is
I stare down at you
like ~~those the~~ a horizon—
the space / the air is between us beckoning
and I am many stories ~~besides~~ up
my feet ~~are~~ frightened
~~from my~~ as I grasp ~~for~~ towards you

Only parts of us will ever touch ~~only~~ parts of others–

Ones own truth is just that really – Ones own truth.

We can only share the part that is ~~acceptable~~ within another's knowing to ~~the~~ other – ~~therefore~~ so one is for most part alone.

As it is meant to be in evidently in nature – at best ~~though~~ perhaps ~~it should~~ could make our understanding seek others loneliness out.

Only parts of us will ever
touch ~~only~~ parts of others—
one's own truth is just
that really—one's own truth.
We can only share the
part that is ~~understood by~~ within another's knowing acceptable ~~to~~
~~the other therefore~~ so one
is for most part alone.
As it is meant to be in
evidently in nature—at best ~~though~~ perhaps it could make
our understanding seek
another's loneliness out.

I can't really stand Human Beings sometimes – I know They all have their problems as I have mine – but I'm really too tired for it. Trying to understand, making allowances, seeing certain things That just weary me.

I can't really stand Human
Beings sometimes—I know
they all have their problems
as I have mine—but I'm really
too tired for it. Trying to understand,
making allowances, seeing certain things
that just weary me.

on Hospital gowns

my bare
classic derrière
is out ~~the~~
in the Air
when I'm not aware
aware
several

Handel Concertos

Vivaldi Concertos

Benny Goodman

My

Last 6 — Beethoven — Quartets

~~Ravel - the waltz~~

Bartok - quartets of his

~~continued on other side~~
of list of records

On Hospital gowns

My bare
(darrie) derrière
is out ~~the air~~
in the air
when I'm not aware
aware
several
Handel Concertos
Vivaldi Concertos
Benny Goodman

My (pair)

Beethoven
Last 6—quartets
Ravel—the Waltz
Bartok—quartets of his
continued on other side
of list of records

stretch
expantion
open free

Beverly Hills Hotel

buy the cake
to begin with a ray tension

Keep the balloon

And

Dare not to worry

Dare to
let go - so loose
Then you pick up
stretch in-to your tone

sense of humor

Keeping a giggle inside

let go of
my eyes -
so relaxed
only let
my thought
come through
Them without
doing any
Thing to
them

stretch
expansion

open free

Keep the
rule
To begin
with
a ray
tension

Keep the balloon
And
Dare not to worry
Dare to
let go—so loose
Then you pick up
Stretch into your tone

Sense of humor
Keeping a giggle inside

Let go of my
eyes—
so relaxed
only let
my thought
come through
them without
doing any
thing to
them

Marilyn in the garden of Hotel Bel-Air, Los Angeles, 1952
Marilyn reading Joyce's *Ulysses*, Long Island, summer of 1955

JAMES JOYCE
ULYSSES

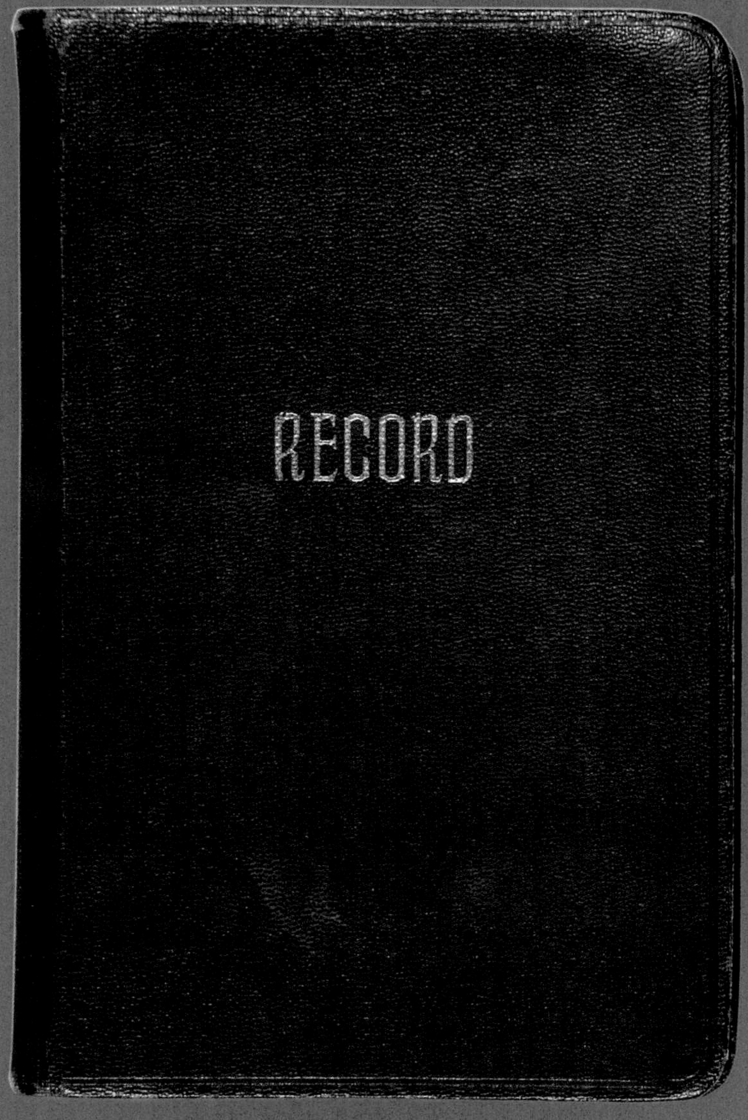
RECORD

"RECORD" BLACK NOTEBOOK

AROUND 1951

As she often did, Marilyn filled only a few pages of this notebook, about twelve out of the hundred and fifty it contains and at obviously distinct periods. The first pages open with a heartfelt "Alone!!!" followed by reflections on fear and feelings that can't be put into words; these were probably jotted down in response to acting classes, which may have been those given by Michael Chekhov that she started attending in September 1951. On page 135 of the notebook, there is a poignant text about the panicky fear that sometimes overtook her when she was about to shoot a scene because of her dread of disappointing; her deep-seated sense that, despite the good work she had done, the bad outweighed it, sapping her confidence. Here the language is very strong: "depressed mad."

On page 146, she jotted down in pencil one of the few lines she delivered in *Love Nest* (1951), a film by Joseph M. Newman, in the supporting but nonetheless crucial role of Roberta Stevens, who was the former wartime (girl?)friend of the hero, Jim Scott.

The notes on pages 148 and 149 of the notebook indicate diligent reading on the Florentine Renaissance, unless they are class notes from courses she attended at UCLA in the fall of 1950, after she had already begun acting in films. However, this school-like exercise is surrounded by an older story that most likely preceded her star status, as she writes of traveling in a crowded bus. Could this have been the same bus in which she met sixty likable Italian sailors, then a headily perfumed Filipino boy, ending up, half-crushed by a sleeping five-year-old almost slipping from his young mother's arms, in the middle of sailors far too young to feel sad?

Alone !!!!!!

I am alone I am always alone

no matter what

Look May
HU 2729 /
Rupert Allen

There is nothing to fear but fear itself

What do I believe in What is truth

I believe in my self
even my most delicate intangible feelings
in the end Everything is intangible

my most precious liquid must never spill don't spill your precious liquid life force

They are all my feelings
no mater what

My feeling doesn't happen to swell into words -

Alone!!!!!
I am alone—I am always
alone
no matter what.

Look Mag
Hu 27291
Rupert Allan

There is nothing to fear
but fear itself

What do I believe in
What is truth
I believe in myself
even my most delicate
intangible feelings
in the end everything is
intangible
my most precious liquid must
never spill don't spill your precious liquid
life force
they are all my feelings
no matter what

My feeling doesn't
happen to swell
into words—

Note: Rupert Allan met Marilyn in 1959. As the West Coast editor of *Look* magazine, he had secured Marilyn her first cover photo, which appeared on June 3, 1952. This may explain her reference "Look Mag." Subsequently, Rupert Allan became Marilyn's press agent and remained such up until the end of the filming of *The Misfits*, when he accepted Grace Kelly's offer to work for her in Monaco.

actress must have no mouth

shoulder girdle hanging
hanging
loose
everything

legit — no feel
focus my thoughts on the partner —
feeling in the end of my fingers

Nothing must come — between me and my part — my feeling concentration

The feeling only getting rid of everything else

my mind speak

letting go — no looks — face — body only feeling

No Attitude

listening to the lady for the feeling.

listen with the eyes

buoyancy

Tension

loose — having no brakes

feeling only — (letting go of everything) All I have to do is think it. How do I hear the melody — the Tone springs from emotion

Tone — groans and moans — "I'm so sick" — ("animals — down to the toes") hums from

with cat — hum — nice kitty

starts from below my feet — All in my feet

what in my body ... how is my head

Actress must have no mouth
no feet
shoulder
girdle hangs light
hanging
so-o-o
loose
everything
focus my thought on
the partner—
feeling in the end of
my fingers

~~Nothing must come
between me and my
part—my feeling—
concentration~~
The feeling only
getting rid of everything
else
my mind speaks
no looks
body only
letting go—face feeling
mind
spirit

no attitude
listening to the body for
the feeling
listen with the eyes
buoyancy
Tension
loose—having no brakes
letting go of everything.
feeling only—all I have to
do is think it. How do
I hear the melody—the
Tone springs from emotion
Tone—groans and moans—"I'm
(animals—"down to the hogs")
so sick"—hums from
with cat—hum—nice kitty soft.

starts from below my feet
feet—all in my feet.

What is my pantomime playing with
How is my head?

4

as if I might never
speak more

5

~~transparency~~

letting go

down down in back

breathing only — pulling up from here

right tension — stomach

as if I might never
speak   move

transparency.
letting go.
down down in back.
pulling up from here.
right tension   stomach
[illegible] only

fear of giving me the lines New
maybe won't be able to learn them
maybe I'll make mistake
people will either think I'm
no good or laugh or
belittle me or think I
can't act
women looked stern and
critical - unfriendly and
cold in general
afraid director can't think I'm
any good -
remembering when I
couldn't do a God damn
thing
After trying to build
myself up with the
fact that I have done
things right that were
even good and have
had moments that
were excellent but
the bad is heavier to
to carry around and
feel before new confidence
depressed mood)

Fear of giving me the lines new
maybe won't be able to learn them
maybe I'll make mistakes
people will either think I'm no good or
laugh or belittle me or think I can't act.
Women looked stern and critical—
unfriendly and cold in general
afraid director won't think I'm any good.
remembering when I couldn't do a god
damn thing.
then trying to build myself up with the
fact that I have done things right that
were even good and have had moments
that were excellent but the bad is heavier
to carry around and feel have no confidence
depressed mad

~~Pardon me~~
~~are you~~ ~~the~~ Janitors
~~Wife~~

caught a greyhound
~~Came~~ Bus from Monterey
to Salinas on the
Bus I was the ~~only~~ person
woman with about
fifty italian fisherman
and I've never ~~met~~
sixty such charming gentleman - they
were wonderful - some
company was sending them
down ~~state~~ where their boats
and fish (they hoped) were
waiting for them. some
couldn't hardly speak english
not only do I love Greeks
~~[illegible]~~ I love Italians -
their ~~[illegible]~~ warm, lusty and Friendly
as hell - I'd love to go to
Italy some day.

Pardon me
are you the janitor's
wife

caught a Greyhound
Bus from Monterey
to Salinas. On the
Bus I was the ~~only~~ person
woman with about
sixty italian fishermen
and I've never met
sixty such charming gentlemen—they
were wonderful. Some
company was sending them
downstate where their boats
and (they hoped) fish were
waiting for them. Some
could hardly speak english
not only do I love Greeks
[illegible] I love Italians.
they're ~~so~~ warm, lusty and friendly
as hell—I'd love to go to
Italy someday.

Notes:
The sentence on page 146 of the notebook is one of the few lines Marilyn had to say in *Love Nest* (1951), so we may assume that these notes—at any rate, the ones written in pencil—date from the same period.

In February 1948, Marilyn went to the California towns of Salinas and Castroville in order to promote diamond sales in two jewelry stores. She stayed at the Jeffery Hotel in Salinas for a week.

148 proto-type - first type Medici 1400 AD-1748

first founding home

Giovanni di Bicci
Bronze doors in the
in Florence
used his Ghiberti 23 perspective 1424
great Architect Brunelleschi 22
Donatello 1386-1466
Masaccio 1401-1428
father of modern art (realistic
poverty careless about his painting)
life except his painting.
Giovanni di Bicci responsible
for him. his work never recognized
until after his death.
The panthon - Temple
Greek philosophy - golden mean
matter too big - too small
kept out old pope
gave money for temples for Brunelleschi
elected him Signoria
Gonfaloniere (governing body)
(pres)

Grande - nobles 149

Giovanni di Bicci
d 1428

Cosimo - (Pater Patriae) Lorenzo
1424 - first Public library

Piero Giovanni
Lorenzo (the Magnificent) Guliano

Machiavelli
1469-1527
Botticelli

Damn near broke my back
and dislocated my neck trying not to [illegible]
trying to sleep in chair
[illegible]
moved my seat where a
lot left ten by the
only empty seat so
I left since the
girl could sit her feet
down and I took the
other seat. It was next
to a philippino boy and
he smelled good like
flowers

Medici 1400 AD–1748
Prototype—first type
Giovanni di Bicci first foundling home
Bronze doors in the
in Florence 1424
Ghiberti 23 perspective
used his great architect
Brunelleschi 22
Donatello 1386–1466
Masaccio 1401–1428
father of modern art (reality
poverty careless about his painting)
life except his painting—
Giovanni di Bicci responsible
for him. His work never recognized
until after his death.
The Pantheon—temple
Greek philosophy—golden mean
(neither too big—or too small)
kept ousted old pope
gave money for temples for Brunelleschi
elected him Signoria
Gonfaloniere (governing body)
(pres)

Grande—nobles

Giovanni di Bicci † 1428

Cosimo (Pater Patriae) — Lorenzo
1424—first public library

Piero — Giovanni

Lorenzo (the Magnificent) — Giuliano

Macchiavelli (1469–1527)
Botticelli

---

damn near broke my back
and dislocated my neck trying not to
sleep all over the filipino boy
Moved my seat when a
[illegible] left the bus—the
only empty seat so
I left mine ~~for~~ so the
girl could sit her kid
down and I took the
other seat. It was next to
a filipino boy and
he smelled good like
flowers.

~~Feb 24 New York~~

I saw a lot of lonely young sailors they who looked too young to be so sad.

they ~~looked like slender~~ reminded me of slender young trees still growing & painful

rude girl next to me for a while she was younger than I with a kid about five that she held as if he were six months — the seat were so small & crowded especially when ~~you~~ the people in front of you push the button for the chairs to recline I slept all over the kid next to me and the kid slept all over me. It was pretty hot except drafty around the windows

and made my ~~throat~~ neck ache

~~pre~~ Feb 24 New-Yorker

I saw a lot of lonely young
sailors who/they looked too
young to be so sad.
They ~~looked like slender~~ reminded me of
young slender trees still
growing & painful

rode—girl next to me for a while she was
younger than I with a kid about five that
she held as if he were six months—the
seats were so small and crowded
especially when the people in front of you
push the button for the chairs to recline
I slept all over the kid next to me and
the kid slept all over me. It was really hot
except drafty around the windows
and made my throat/neck ache

Marilyn with a book about Goya, around 1953
Marilyn and Degas sculpture, Los Angeles, 1956

RECORD

OTHER "RECORD" NOTEBOOK

AROUND 1955

This black notebook has a smoother cover than the preceding one. Only the first few pages have been filled; pages 3 and 4 have disappeared, because Marilyn either ripped out the sheet to write on, or did so on rereading it. It is likely that this group of notes, which is coherent and forms a certain continuity, dates from the time Marilyn started working with Lee Strasberg, around 1955. A sincere effort at introspection can be observed as the star returned to her childhood and the lifelong fears it engendered. Aunt Ida is probably Ida Martin (rather than Ida Bolender, with whom Marilyn also stayed as a child). Ida Martin was the mother of Marilyn's aunt by marriage, an evangelical Christian and strict disciplinarian who emphasized obedience and was repressive about sexual issues in general; she may also have made the twelve-year-old Norma Jeane feel guilty for an episode in which she said she had been molested.

To no longer feel ashamed of what you were, of what you desired: this was what Marilyn, who had made her childhood dream come true by becoming an actress, was now aiming for. We may also assume that she had just started psychoanalysis, as she pointed out the bent of the unconscious to forget and repress, an impulse she urged herself to struggle against by trying to reclaim memory in order to be able to accept herself fully.

She experienced work as a way of freeing herself from the constraints and shackles of the past, and these pages can be read as an outline of self-analysis, both gripping and moving.

Life starts from Now

Ida – I have still been obeying her – its not only harmful (inhibits myself, " my work, " thoughts) for me to do so but unreality because

In my work – I don't want to obey her any longer and I can do my work as fully as I wish since as a small child in fact first desire was to be an actress

I have and spent years play acting until I had jobs

I will not be punished

cont. page 8

or trying to hide it

enjoying myself as fully as I wish or want to

I will be as sensitive as I am – without being ashamed of it

trust in the faith in the simple objects and tasks – (Sense Memory – outside and inside objects)

I haven't had Faith in Life meaning Reality – what ever it is or happens

There is nothing to hold on to – but reality.

To realize the present what ever it may be – because that's how it is and its much better life starts from now

Ida—I have still
been obeying her—
it's not only harmful
for me to do so
but unrealality because

(inhibits myself
inhibits my work
inhibits thoughts)

In my work—I don't
want to obey her any longer
and I can do my work as fully
as I wish since as a small child
intact first desire was to be an actress
and I spent years
play acting until I had jobs
I have
I will not be punished
[cont. page 8]
or trying to hide it
enjoying myself as fully
as I wish or want to
I will be as sensitive as
I am—without being ashamed of it

trust in the
faith in the simple
objects and tasks—(sense
memory—outside and inside
objects)
I haven't had Faith in Life
meaning Reality—what
ever it is or happens
There is nothing to
hold on to—but reality
to realize the present
what ever it may be
—because that's how it
is and it's much better >>>

6

to Know Reality (or things as they are than ~~to have~~ not to know and to have few illusions as possible—

7

Train my will now

>>> to know reality (or
things as they are than
~~to have~~ not to know
and to have few
illusions as possible—

train my will now

8

working (doing my tasks that I have set for myself) on the stage - I will not be punished for it
or be whipped
" " threatened
or not be loved
or sent to hell to burn with bad people
~~or~~ feeling that I am also bad.
or be afraid of my genitals being ~~exposed~~ known and seen -
or ashamed
~~or~~ (ashamed of my sensitivity) (feelings - they are reality) So what! or colors or screaming or doing nothing
I do have feeling
very strongly sexed feeling since a small child - Think of all the things I felt then

9

I do know ways people act unconventually - mainly myself - do not be afraid of my sensitivity or to use it - for I (can + will channel it) - crazy thoughts too (useful however idiotic as they seem)
I want to do my scene or exercise as sincerely as I can knowing and showing how I know, it is also - no matter - what they might think - or judge from it

working (doing my tasks that I
have set for myself)
On the stage—I will
not be punished for it
or be whipped
or be threatened
or not be loved
or sent to hell to burn with bad people
~~or~~ feeling that I am also bad.
or be afraid of my genitals being
or ashamed
exposed known and seen—
so what
or ashamed of my sensitive feelings—
they are reality
or colors or screaming or doing
nothing
and I do have feeling
very strongly sexed feeling
since a small child—(think of all the
things I felt then

I do know ways people
act unconventionally—mainly
myself—do not be afraid of
my sensitivity or to use it—for I
can & will channel it + crazy thoughts too
I want to do my scene or exercises
([illegible] idiotic as they seem)
as sincerely as ~~possible~~ I
can knowing and showing
how I know it is also—no
matter—what they might
think—or judge from it

I can and will help
my self and work on
things analitically no
matter how painful - if I
forget things (the unconsise wants to
forget - I will only try to remember)
Discipline - Concentration

my body is my body
every part of it.

I can and will help
myself and work on
things analytically no
matter how painful—if I
forget things (the unconscious
wants to
forget—I will only try to remember)
Discipline—Concentration

my body is my body
every part of it.

feel what I feel
within myself – that is,
become aware of it, trying to
also what I feel in others
not being ashamed of my
feelings, thoughts – or ideas

realize the thing that
they are –

feel what I feel
within myself—that is trying to
become aware of it
also what I feel in others
not being ashamed of my
feeling, thoughts—or ideas

realize the thing <u>that</u>
they are—

when I start to feel sudenly depressed what does it come from (in reality) trace incidents. maybe to ex past time - feeling guilty?

realize all the sensitivity aspects. not being ashamed of what ever I feel (don't dismiss this lightly either)

not regretting saying what I've said if it is really true to me even when it is not under stood - don't even try to convince anyone to much as to why - unless I really want to - or really feel it.

tension - where do I feel it be aware of it (where do I think I comes from)

conciously make effort to relax brows
temples
area around mouth.
cheek
collapse shoulders
jaws
{changing loose}

make effort to be aware - like when feeling sick - try to stop chain reaction before it gets started if it does start - dont worry realize it be aware of it, concioualy making the effort

When I start to
feel suddenly depressed
what does it come from
(in reality) trace incidents
maybe to
ex past time—feeling guilty?
realize all the sensitivity
aspects. not being ashamed
of whatever I feel
don't dismiss
this lightly either
not regretting saying
what I've said if it
is really true to me
<u>even</u> when it is not
understood—(don't even
try to convince anyone too
much as to why—unless I
really want to—or really feel it.

tension—<u>where</u> do
<u>I feel it be aware of it</u> <u>what/where</u> do I
<u>think it comes from</u>
Consciously make effort to
relax brows
temples
<u>area around</u> mouth.

collapse
cheek shoulders hanging
jaws <u>loose</u>

make effort to be
aware—like when feeling
sick—try to stop chain reaction
before it gets started if
it does start—don't worry
realize it be aware of it
consciously making the effort

16

having a sense of myself.

17

having a sense of myself

Marilyn reading *To the Actor* by Michael Chekhov, New York, 1955
Marilyn writing at home, May 1953

WALDORF-ASTORIA STATIONERY

1955

Marilyn Monroe's immense popular appeal had at last been recognized by the Hollywood elite, who had gathered together at a party given in her honor by Charles Feldman, the producer of *The Seven Year Itch*, on November 6, 1954, at the Beverly Hills Romanoff. Still dissatisfied with what Hollywood had to offer, Marilyn decided to leave the West Coast for New York and set up Marilyn Monroe Productions with the photographer Milton Greene. This was a tremendous challenge to the all-powerful studios and a gesture for which she would never really be fully forgiven. From then on her life would swing between the West Coast and the East Coast, a contest between the movie-star image and the cultural and artistic self-invention that the Actors Studio and her New York acquaintances made possible. After a few weeks spent at the Gladstone Hotel, she stayed in a three-room suite on the twenty-seventh floor of the Waldorf-Astoria from April to September 1955. The following documents were written on this prestigious hotel's stationery. They include a long prose poem, the account of a nightmarish dream that is full of surprises (not least her drama teacher turning into a surgeon), thoughts and notes about what Lee Strasberg had said (she misspelled his name with a double "s") during the classes she attended at the Actors Studio, the draft of a letter to a certain "Claude," and a list of song titles. Some of these documents are discontinuous, and the links between texts, which might have been written in any order, have been left to the reader's discernment.

O sad, sweet trees—
I wish for you—rest
but you must be wakeful

What was that now—
Just a moment ago—
from it was mine and
now its gone—like the
swift movement of a moment
gone—
maybe I'll remember
because it felt
as though it
started to be ~~wonder~~—
~~felt~~—mine

The Towers of
THE WALDORF-ASTORIA
NEW YORK
ELDORADO 5-3100

So poor
So many—
lights in the darkness
making skeletons of Buildings
and life in the streets

What ~~was it~~ were
~~I~~ the things I thought about only yesterday
~~down~~ in the streets?—
~~Now~~ Seem so far away (~~up here~~) Long ago
and ~~a~~ moon ~~so full and dark~~
Its better ~~I learned~~ they told me as a child what it was
for I could not guess it or understand it

now—
noises ~~from~~ of impatience from cab drivers always driving—who
must drive—Hot, dusty, ~~snowing~~ icy streets so they
can eat, and perhaps save for a vacation, in which they
~~will~~ can drive their wives all the way accross the
country to see her relatives—
the part of the river made of pesi cola—the park—Thank god for the park,
Yet I am not looking at these things
I'm looking for my lover

its good they told me what
the moon was when I was a child

then the river—
The part made of
pepsi cola—

Sad, sweet trees—
I wish for you—rest
but you must be wakeful

What was that now—
just a moment ago—
from it was mine and
now it's gone—like the
swift movement of a moment
gone—
maybe I'll remember
because it felt
as though it
started to be ~~wonderful~~
~~only~~ mine

Sooooo many lights in the darkness
making skeletons of buildings
and life in the streets
~~The things~~ What ~~were~~ was it I thought about yesterday
~~down~~ in the streets?
It ~~now~~ seems so far away ~~up here~~ long ago
and moon ~~so full and dark~~.
It's better ~~I learned~~ they told me as a child what it was
for I could not ~~guess it~~ ~~or~~ understand it now.
Noises ~~from~~ of impatience from cab drivers always driving who
must drive—hot, dusty, ~~snowing~~ icy streets so they
can eat, and perhaps save for a vacation, in which they
~~will~~ can drive their wives all the way across the
country to see her relatives.
Then the river—the part made of pepsi cola—the park—thank god for the park
Yet I am not looking at these things
I'm looking for my lover
It's good they told me what
the moon was when I was a child. >>>

That silent ~~stirring~~ river which stirs
and swells itself with what ever passes over it
wind rain, great ships never unmoved
I love the river—
by any thing
Its quite now
And the silience is alone
except for the thunderous rumbling of things unknown distant drums. very present
but for the screems and the whispers of things
sharp sounds and percincing of and then suddenly hushed
to moans beyond sadness— terror beyond
fear
The cry of things dim and too young to be known yet
the sobs of life itself
that
and bear the pain & the Joy
of newness on your limbs

Loneliness— be still

You must suffer—
~~to loose your dark golden~~
when your covering of
even dead leaves leave you
strong and Naked—
you must be—
alive— when looking dead
straight though bent
with wind

>>> That silent ~~stirring~~ river which stirs
and swells itself with whatever passes over it
wind, rain, great ships.
I love the river—~~it is~~ never unmoored
by anything
It's quiet now
And the silence is alone
except for the thunderous rumbling of things unknown
distant drums very present
but for the piercing of screams
and the whispers of things
sharp sounds and then suddenly hushed
to moans beyond sadness—terror beyond
fear
The cry of things dim and too young to be known yet
The sobs of life itself

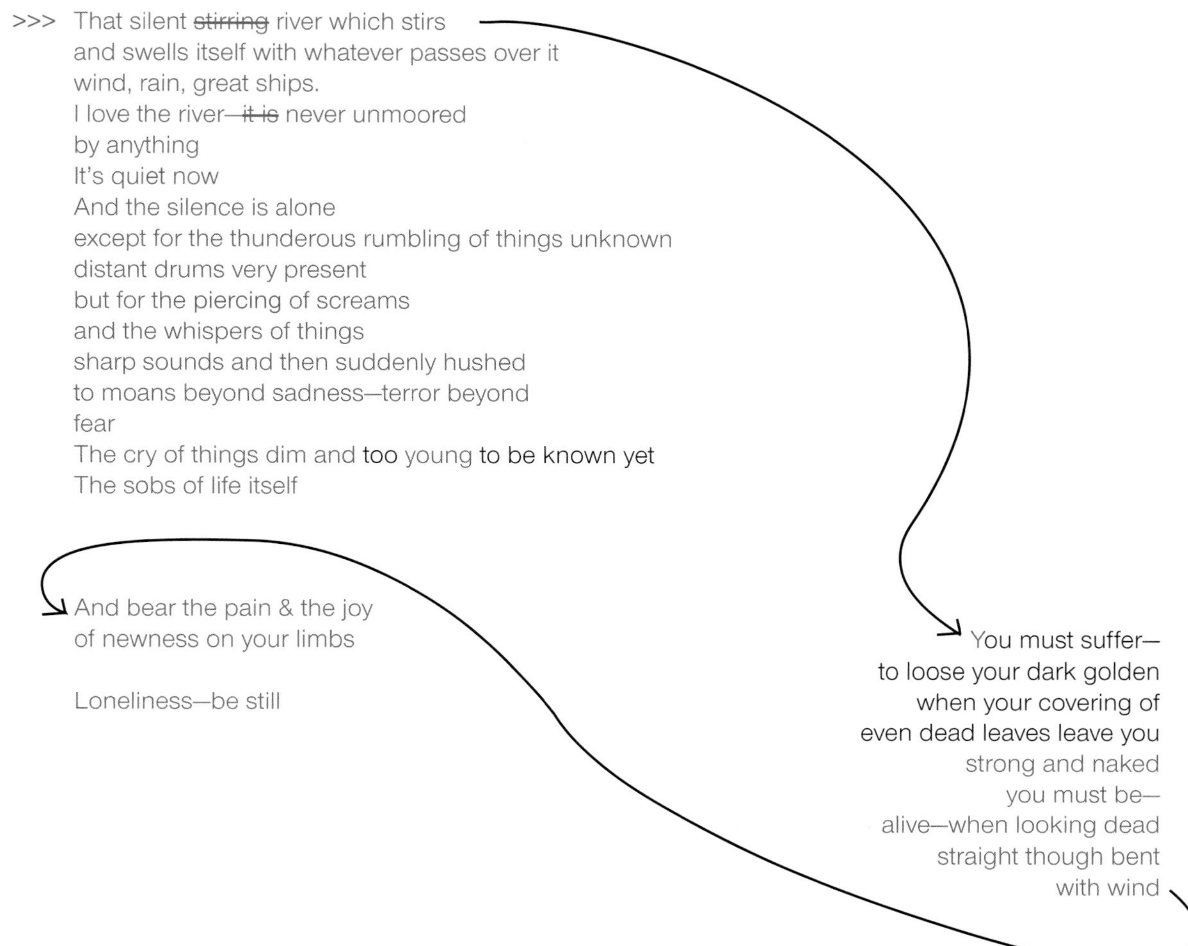

You must suffer—
to loose your dark golden
when your covering of
even dead leaves leave you
strong and naked
you must be—
alive—when looking dead
straight though bent
with wind

And bear the pain & the joy
of newness on your limbs

Loneliness—be still

(1)

The Towers of THE WALDORF-ASTORIA
NEW YORK
ELDORADO 5-3100

make no more promyses ~~explanations~~ As—if—possible
" " Regarding Anne Karger
after this make no commitments of tie my self down to engagments in future—to save not being able to keep them and mostly to avoid feeling guilty which is now the case

best finest surgeon—Strassberg to cut me open ~~which~~ which I dont mind since Dr. H. has prepared me—given me anesetic and has also dyanosed the case and agrees with what has to be done—an operation—to bring myself back to life and to cure me of this terrible dis-ease what ever the hell it is—

~~A~~rthur—is the only one waiting in the outer room—worring & hoping operation succesful for many reasons—for myself—for his play and for himself indirectly

Hedda—Concerned—keeps calling on phone during operation—Norman—keeps stopping by hospital to see if Im okay but mostly to comfort Art who is so worried—

Milton calls from big office with lots of room and every thing in good taste—and is conducting business in a new way with style—and music is playing and he is relaxed and engoying himself even if he is very worried at the same time—theres a camera on his desk but he doesnt take pictures anymore except of great paintings.

Strassberg cuts me open after Dr. H. gives me

Make no more promises
make no more
explanations—if possible.
Regarding Anne Karger
after this make no
commitments or tie
myself down to engagements
in future—to save
not being able to keep
them and mostly to
avoid feeling guilty
which is now the
case.

Best finest surgeon—Strasberg
~~waits~~ to cut me open which I don't mind since Dr. H
has prepared me—given me anesthetic
and has also diagnosed the case and
agrees with what has to be done—
an operation—to bring myself back to
life and to cure me of this terrible dis-ease
whatever the hell it is—
Arthur is the only one waiting in the outer
room—worrying and hoping operation successful
for many reasons—for myself—for his play and
for himself indirectly
Hedda—concerned—keeps calling on phone during
operation—Norman—keeps stopping by hospital to
see if I'm okay but mostly to comfort Art
who is so worried—
Milton calls from big office with lots of room
and everything in good taste—and is conducting
business in a new way with style—and music
is playing and he is relaxed and enjoying himself even if he
is very worried at the same time—there's a camera
on his desk but he doesn't take pictures anymore except
of great paintings.
Strasberg cuts me open after Dr. H gives me

>>>

Notes:

Anne Karger was the mother of the man sometimes identified as Marilyn's first real love, Fred Karger, whom she met in 1948 when he was a (then-married) voice coach at Columbia Pictures. She stayed on good terms with Anne all her life.

Dr. H. refers to Dr. Margaret Hohenberg (see page 201).

Hedda Rosten had been a close friend of Marilyn's since 1955 and became her personal assistant for a time. Norman was Hedda's husband.

"Art" was one of the nicknames Marilyn gave to Arthur Miller.

Milton Greene took many photos of Marilyn before becoming her business partner.

for Dr. H. tell about that dream of the horrible repulsive man – who is trying to lean to close to me in elevator – and my panic and then my thought of despising him – does that mean I'm attracted to him – he even looks like he has a venera dassese

The Towers of
THE WALDORF-ASTORIA
NEW YORK
ELDORADO 5-3100

Anesithea and trys in a medical way to comfort me – everything in the room is white infact I can't even see anyone just white objects –

they cut me open – Strassberg with Hohenbergs ass. and there is absolutly nothing there – strassberg is deeply disapointed but more even – academically amazed that he had made such a mistake He thought there was going to be so much – more than he had ever dreamed possible in almost anyone but in stead there was absolutly nothing – devoid of every human living feeling thing – the only thing that came out was so finely cut sawdust – like out of a raggady ann doll – and the sawdust spills all over the floor & table and Dr. H. is puzzled because sudenly she realizes that this is a new type case – the ~~patient~~ (pupil or student – I started to write) existing of complete emptyness

Strassbergs dreams & hopes for theater are fallen
D. H's ______ " " a permant phycatreic cure is given up – Arthurs – is disappointed – let down +

For Dr H.
tell about that
dream of the horrible
repulsive man—who is trying to
lean too close to me in
elevator—and my panic
and then all my thought
despising him—does that mean
I'm attached
to him

>>> anesthesia and tries in a medical way to comfort
me—everything in the room is white in fact I
can't even see anyone just white objects—
they cut me open—Strasberg with Hohenberg's ass.
and there is absolutely nothing there—Strasberg is
deeply disappointed but more even—academically amazed
that he had made such a mistake. He thought there was going
to be so much—more than he had ever dreamed possible in
almost anyone but
instead there was absolutely nothing—devoid of
every human living feeling thing—the only thing
that came out was so finely cut sawdust—like
out of a raggedy ann doll—and the sawdust spills
all over the floor & table and Dr. H is puzzled
because suddenly she realizes that this is a
new type case ~~of puple~~. The patient (pupil—or student—I started to write) existing
of complete emptiness
Strasberg's dreams & hopes for theater are fallen.
Dr. H's dreams and hopes for a permanent psychiatric cure
is given up—Arthur is disappointed—let down +

He even looks
like he has
a venereal
disease.

why did it mean so much to me when after all that crying sobbing on stage - He said when I was kind of

I want you all to know that this exercise went on for ½ hr. and her concentration did not give way or slip once - and Marilyn here will be very few times ever on the stage where it will be necessary to keep such a concentration for one half hour - straight.

The Towers of
THE WALDORF-ASTORIA
NEW YORK
ELDORADO 5-3100

~~Dear Art,~~
~~Don't overwork - keep well~~

reaction - I'm always afraid when so one praises me it's even worse in its own peculiar way (the way in that particular way) it makes me suffer with such misgivings - that the whole thing is an accident even probably it wasn't me at all

everyone has violence in themselves
I am violent -

time with it, away either and not waste dealing with fear not running deeper changes - which is (mean) from fear into the your sensitivity to turn to be done - to deal with Remember - technical things can from. That - fear and fear alone into just fear and acting only effects (turning your fear against yourself) whole thing backwards

most people in this country take it the opposite way you do and that's why (partly I put that in) some people you know admire you - just for that

but your sensitivity would not be the same if you didnt have these fearful misgiving? - which from your experiences (past) you reacted but technically you will be able to handle it not get rid of it.

Why did it
mean so much to
me when after all that
crying sobbing on
stage—he said when
I was kind of

I want you all to know
that this exercise went on for
½ hour and her concentration did not
give way or slip once—and Marilyn there
will be very few times ever on the
stage where it will be
necessary to keep
such a concentration
for one half hour
straight.

~~Dear Art,~~
~~Don't overwork—keep well~~

reaction (—I'm always afraid when someone praises me it's even
worse in its own peculiar way in that particular way it makes me
suffer with such misgivings)—that the whole thing is an
accident even probably it wasn't me at all

everyone has violence in themselves. I am violent.

most people in this country
take it the opposite way you
do and that's why (partly I put that in) some people
you know admire you—just for
that

but your sensitivity
would not be the same
if you didn't have these
fearful misgivings?—which
from your experience (past) you've reacted but
technically you will be
able to handle it
not get rid of it
without dangerous effects

whole thing backwards
(turning your fear against yourself)
into just fear and acting only
from that—fear and fear alone
Remember—technical things can
to be done—to deal with
your sensitivity to turn
it from fear into the
proper channels—which is (means)
dealing with fear, not running
away either and not waste
time with it.

not a scared, lonely little girl anymore) → Remember — your sitting on top of the world, (it doesnt feel like it) you own have any help you want — personally — or in your work — or anything else you want — too much talent

too much ability — There are tecnical ways to go about it or problems — figure out if anything tec. can be done about it because there are people to help you — gladly — more than most they want to help

and much too much sensitivity to invert yourself

out of fear — not coming to class — or to do things like being afraid to come to class or to get up — remember there is nothing you lack — nothing to be self concious about yourself — you have everything but the disapline and tecnick which you are learning & seeking

like susie — where ever you are there is a kind of light about you — no acting can give you this quality. — on your own — after all nothing was or is being given to you you have had none of this worth throwin your way — you seeked it it didn't seek you

the sensitivity is so strong — much deeper and stronger than that of susies

In fact the sensitivity is so full and so strong it is dangerous because — the emotions can also rule everything. most cases there is not the emotional

He feels I will be able for my first part to really be a tremendous part which is rare — like in the case of suzie | Her background different surprising disapline (self developed) she posses so young

exposure — embarrising —

The best actors Duse had it that sometimes she wouldnt play not that she couldnt but didnt wish to expose herself in her then present state

my fear is not illogical only its illogical at this time — dont work out of it — tecnical devises will help my concentration.

to overcome the difficulties — Remember the fear is always there and will be in your case But there is something you can do about it technically | which by only making the effort by carrying out the tec-nical exercises. (putting them together — there is a scene.)

Strassberg (Him he said)

it makes me feel badly (and sadly) for you that you do ~~practically every~~ things out of fear.

You must start to do things out of strength — (my question) where do I get the strength) — he said — by not looking for strength but only looking & seeking tecnical ways and means

Remember you(r) can sit~~ting~~ on top of the world (it doesn't feel like it).
You can have any help you want personally—or in your
work—or anything else you want—
There are technical ways to go about it
or problems—figure out if anything tec. can be done
about it because there are people to help you—gladly—you
more than most they want to help
Remember there is nothing you
lack—nothing to be self conscious about
yourself—you have everything but the discipline
and technique which you are learning & seeking
on your own—
after all nothing was or
is being given to you—
you have had none of this
work thrown your way
you sought it
—it didn't seek you

Not a scared
lonely little girl
anymore

Too much talent
Too much ability and
and much too much sensitivity to invert yourself
out of fear—not come to class—
or to do things like being afraid to come to
class or to get up.

Like Susie—where you are wherever you walk there is a kind of light about
you—no acting can give you this quality.
The sensitivity is so strong—much deeper and stronger than that
of Susie's.
In fact the sensitivity is so full and so strong it is dangerous
because the emotions can & do rule everything—most cases there is not the emotional.
He feels I will be able for my first part to really be a tremendous part
which is rare—like in the case of Susie. Her background different
surprisingly discipline (self-developed) she possessed so young.
Exposure—embarrassing.
The best actors. Duse had it that sometimes she wouldn't play (not that
she couldn't but didn't wish to expose herself in her then present state

my fear is not illogical only it's illogical at this time—don't work out
of it—technical devices will help my concentration.

to overcome the difficulties Remember the fear is always there and will be
in your case. But there is something you can do about it
technically which by only making the effort, by carrying out the
technical exercises (putting them together—there is a scene)

Strasberg
it makes me (him he said) feel badly (and sadly) for you that you do
~~practically every~~ things out of fear
You must start to do things out of strength—
(my question: where do I get the strength)—he said—by not looking for strength
but only looking & seeking technical ways and means

Note: Susie was the nickname of Lee and Paula Strasberg's daughter, born in 1938. At the time she knew Marilyn, she had started a career as a theater actress and also attended the Actors Studio.

please don't talk about me when I'm gone

You're an old smoothie

Body and Soul

Who's Sorry now

easy living

when I'm not near the Boy I love 259

While we're young 262

I know where I'm going and who's going with me?

I cried for you

You do something

the gentleman is a dope

I'll never be the same

He's funny that way

too Marvelous for words

Don't worry about me

What is there to say

But not for me

Easy to Love

Have you ever been lonely

I've got you under my skin

Please don't talk about me when I'm gone
You're an old smoothie
Body and soul?
Who's sorry now
Easy living
When I'm not near the boy I Love 259
While we're young 262
I know where I'm going and who's going with me?
I cried for you
You do something
The gentleman is a dope
I'll never be the same
He's funny that way
too marvelous for words
Don't worry about me
What is there to say
But not for me
Easy to love
Have you ever been lonely
I've got you under my skin

Note: This is a set of song titles. Numbers 259 and 262 are the corresponding numbers to a fake book, or an anthology of lyrics and chord progressions from which musicians could improvise. It is not known why Marilyn made this list; possibly they were songs she wished to perform.

Dear Claude, Claude

thats right—I know exactly what I'm doing and I know
I've just written ~~Dear~~ Claude, Claude — Meanwhile besides

at course its simpler to be a member of The Mr. Johnson club because in knowing from one

where one could probably for stress or strain for exertion is get kicked out of the club probably forbidden

Hope you've — if you haven't come back from Port Jefferson yet — why don't you. Your needed here.

is this true that I ask this question as a member in good standing but there how is it
Am I under the right impression as a Borderline Anonymous one to know since there are no rules
also as a newly chartered member of The Mr. Johnson club Its easier even to be a member of the M.J. club where for any kind of exertion stress or strain your kicked out.

P.S. In a few short days I'm sending you a reminder — to remind you of [illegible] time mostly

This might ~~very well~~ serve as the (a good joke) watchword for some other weekend don't you think
or
do you think I've gone to far

Re-Reminder

The Towers of
THE WALDORF-ASTORIA
NEW YORK
ELDORADO 5-3100

84 Remsen St,
Brooklyn
Chief

Dear Claude Claude,
That's right—I know exactly what I'm doing and I know ~~mean~~
I've just written ~~Dear~~ Claude, Claude—
~~it's because~~ meanwhile besides
"The way of a country man is hard, his training strict, his progress slow, his disappointments many." If in fact he is to ~~survive~~ succeed he must ~~should~~ "give it up." Are you prepared? I am interested only per one "borderline" to the other.
in knowing from one of course it's ~~easier~~ simpler to be a member of the Mr. Johnson club because for when one could probably get kicked out of the club for stress, ~~or~~ strain or **exertion** as probably forbidden—
but then how is one to know
since there are no rules
I ask this question as a member of good standing of Borderline Anonymous also as a newly chartered member of the Mr. Johnson club.
It's easier even to be a member of the M.J. Club where for any kind of exertion, stress or strain you're kicked out.
Is it/this true that I am under the right impression
My love to Hedda and Patty and Candy and Bammoo. Come back if you haven't come back from Port Jefferson yet (hope you've)—why don't you.
You're needed here.
looking forward to seeing you all
Love
Marilyn

P.S. In a few short days I'm sending you a reminder—to remind you ~~of something~~
of me mostly

This might ~~very well~~ serve as
(the)/(a) possible watchword for some
other weekend don't you think
or
do you think I've gone too far

Re—reminder [drawing of envelope]

84 Remsen St.
Brooklyn
Heights

Notes:
Marilyn nicknamed her friend Norman Rosten "Claude" because he looked so much like the actor Claude Rains. He and his wife, Hedda, had a daughter called Patricia (Patty). At this time they lived in Brooklyn, at 84 Remsen Street.

Bam-Moo and Candy were the names of the Rostens' dog and cat.

The Mr. Johnson club was invented by Norman Rosten and Marilyn; the name refers to Rosten's play *Mister Johnson*, based on Joyce Cary's novel, which embodied for Marilyn the spirit of innocence destroyed by cynicism and greed.

On the balcony of the Ambassador Hotel, New York, 1955
Marilyn Monroe with Truman Capote, New York, 1955

ITALIAN AGENDA

1955 or 1956

In an Italian diary engraved in green, Marilyn Monroe wrote down thoughts in free association in continuation of a kind of self-analysis she had begun to practice in the "Record" notebook (she noticed with amusement her own Freudian slip when she wrote the first three letters of the name "Buddy" as "Bad"). It isn't really known who the woman with big breasts was: perhaps her analyst, Dr. Hohenberg (mentioned on another page)? A salaried member of her circle? In any case, Marilyn remembered two traumatic moments: as a lonely child, when, despite the lies she told, a teacher was one of the only people who seemed to understand her; and an incident of sexual abuse for which Ida Martin, her foster mother, seemed to have taken her to task rather than consoling or helping her. It is likely that these pages correspond to work on repressed memory undertaken as part of her analysis with Dr. Hohenberg, which she started in February 1955. Her relationship with her third husband, Arthur Miller, seemed to be idyllic still, propelled as it was by strong desire and absolute confidence: there is no trace of either doubt or crisis.

She also evoked her relationship to fear, which she seemed to need to draw on for her acting but which terrorized her as well. The Peter whom she mentions twice as a source of fear and threat could well be Peter Lawford, whom she knew in the early 1950s, although it is not known with what degree of intimacy. Lawford later became John Kennedy's brother-in-law upon his marriage to Patricia Kennedy. Some years later Marilyn often saw the Lawford couple and visited their Santa Monica beach house several times.

Big Bosom women?

MATTINA POMERIGGIO SERA

DOM.

LUN.

MAR.

MER.

GIOV.

VEN.

SAB.

I'm afraid to ever say anything about her for fear she will think I am trying to flatter her—thereby trying to trap her into liking me

maybe thats why I told the teacher all those lies all the times

Young and dark she was—seemed to believe me even when I wasn't telling the truth—she was curious & it seemed use to ask from time to time to take out

I know it isn't for her trust I primarily pay her for—it really her help and then in trying to get help it naturally pays for trust but then there is some accademic it—like school—

I must ask her why I use to lye to my first grade teacher about her and uncle wayne & nancy about pushing nancy against the stove—may be I was getting even in the only way because nobody else listened to me and that teacher

because she
seemed so interested
in them and seemed
to talk to me + like me
may be I didn't want
her to treat me like Aunt Ida
did -

	MATTINA	POMERIGGIO	SERA
DOM.			
LUN.			
MAR.			
MER.			
GIOV.			
VEN.			
SAB.			

Prodotti Flex mod. 854

Big Bosom Women?

I'm afraid to ever say
anything about her
for fear she will think I
am trying to flatter her—thereby
trying to trap her into liking me

I know it isn't for
her trust I primarily
pay her for—it really **is**
her help and then in
trying to get help it
naturally pays for trust
but then there is some
academic **in** it—like school—
I must ask her why I use**d** to l**i**e
to my first grade teacher about
her and uncle wayne & nancy
about pushing nancy against the
stove—maybe I was getting
even in the only way that
because nobody else
listened to me
and that
teacher

Young and dark she
was—seemed to be-
lieve me even when
I wasn't telling the
truth—she was
curious about
it I sensed &
use**d** to ask
from time
to time later
on—

Maybe that's
why I told
the teacher
all those
lies all
the time

because she
seemed so interested
in them and seemed
to talk to me & like me
maybe I didn't want
her to treat me like Aunt Ida
did—

Note: Ida Bolender and her husband, Albert Wayne, cared for Norma Jeane at their home in Hawthorne from June 1926, shortly after her birth, and she stayed with them until she was seven. The child called Ida Wayne's husband "Daddy" despite the fact that Ida Bolender would have preferred her to call him "Uncle Wayne." The Bolenders adopted two children: Nancy, who was five years younger, and Lester, who was the same age as Marilyn.

I am so concerned
about protecting Arthur
I love him - and he is the
only person - human being I have only
ever known that I could love that I
as a man to which I am attracted to practically
out of my senses about - but he the only
person - as another human being that I trust as
much as myself - because when I do trust my-
-self (about certain things) I do fully and
do about him also -

Peter wants - and I think

- where as woman - and I think
to be a woman - I
would like to be me -

also I trust Dr H.
though in a different
way since I have to pay
her first however

in fact now I think I know
why he's been here so long
because I have a need to
be frighten - and talking really
in my personal relationships (and dealings) lately
have been frightening me - except
for him - I felt very uneasy at different
times with him - the real reason
I was afraid of him - is because I believe
him to be homosexual - not in the
way I have a respect and admiration
who I feel feels I have talent
and wouldn't be jealous
of me because I wouldn't
really want to
be me

why is it I have a feeling—things are not really happening—but I'm playing a part—for which I feel guilty in as much as I know ~~what its~~ premeditated what I'm saying and the effect—excep

← the feeling of violence I've had lately

I'm too inhibited to feel spontaneous I'm afraid— ~~because~~ to be I mean because I don't know what will come out—what will happen

about being afraid of ~~her~~ he might harm me—poison me etc. why—strange look in his eyes—strange behavior

maybe someone will read it? I don't think so

even gas ~~on~~ my stomach ~~afraid~~ fart to write

← even physically I was always sure some was wrong with me. There—

~~afraid~~ to say above but I know where

and I will be humiliated and feel lower than anything or anyone

in other words I'm the worst why?

why do I feel this torture? or why do I feel ~~less~~ than other of a human being than other I always so often felt in a way that I'm sub-human why

I am so concerned
about protecting Arthur
I love him—and he is the
only person—human being I have
ever known that I could love not only
as a man to which I am attracted to practically
out of my senses about—but he is the only
person—as another human being that I trust as
much as myself—because when I do trust myself (about certain things) I do fully, and I
do about him also—

also I trust Dr. H.
though in a different
way since I have to pay
her for it however

whereas Peter wants
to be a woman—and
would like to be me—I think

in fact now I think I know
why he's been here so long
because I have a need to
be frighten—and nothing really
in my personal relationships (and dealings) lately
have been frightening me—except
for him—I felt very uneasy at different
times with him—the real reason
I was afraid of him—is because I believe
him to be homosexual—not in the
way I love & respect and admire Jack
who I feel feels I have talent
and wouldn't be jealous
of me because I wouldn't
really want to
be me

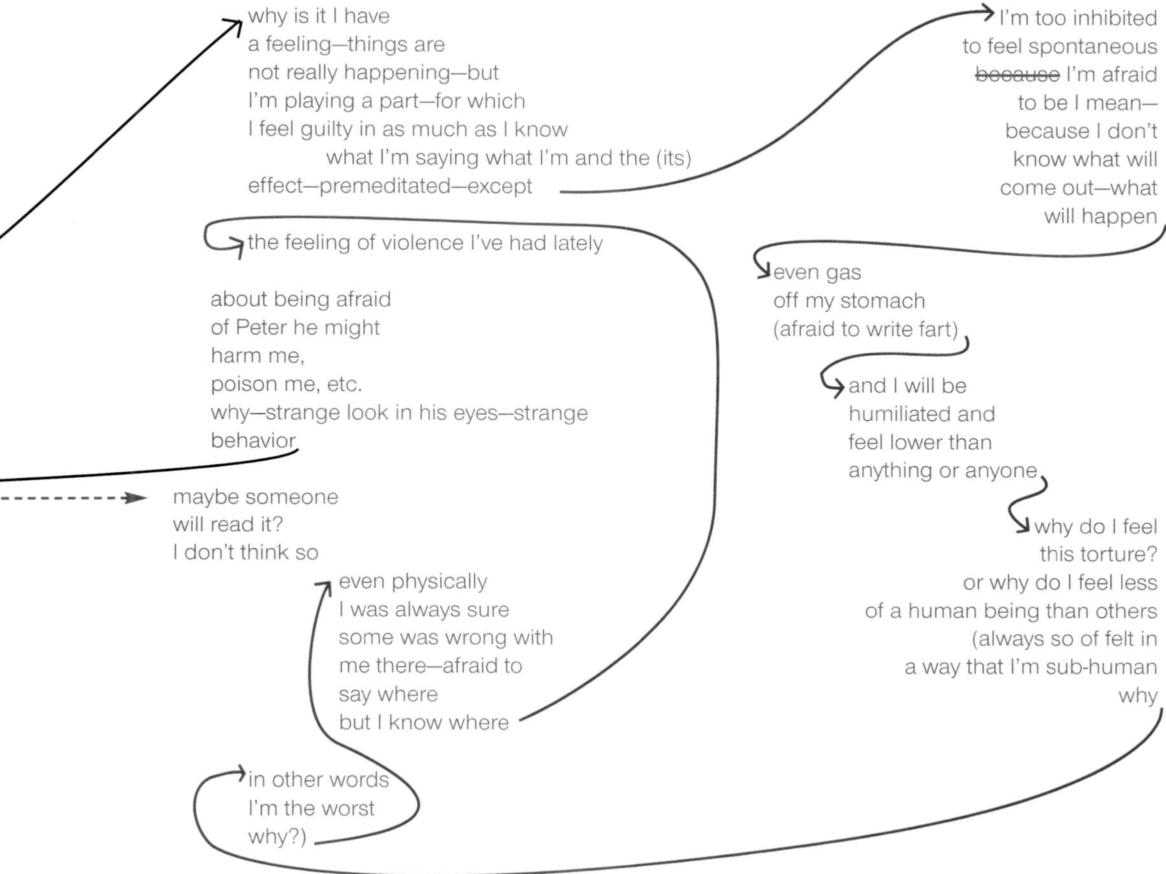

why is it I have
a feeling—things are
not really happening—but
I'm playing a part—for which
I feel guilty in as much as I know
what I'm saying what I'm and the (its)
effect—premeditated—except

I'm too inhibited
to feel spontaneous
~~because~~ I'm afraid
to be I mean—
because I don't
know what will
come out—what
will happen

even gas
off my stomach
(afraid to write fart)

and I will be
humiliated and
feel lower than
anything or anyone

why do I feel
this torture?
or why do I feel less
of a human being than others
(always so of felt in
a way that I'm sub-human
why

in other words
I'm the worst
why?)

even physically
I was always sure
some was wrong with
me there—afraid to
say where
but I know where

the feeling of violence I've had lately

about being afraid
of Peter he might
harm me,
poison me, etc.
why—strange look in his eyes—strange
behavior

maybe someone
will read it?
I don't think so

Notes:
The Peter who is mentioned is possibly the British-born actor Peter Lawford, a friend of Marilyn's and brother-in-law to the Kennedys through his marriage to Pat, the president's sister.

If indeed it is the name "Jack" that is written (the writing is difficult to decipher), it could refer to Jack Cole, a dancer friend of Marilyn's who coached her on the films *Gentlemen Prefer Blondes* and *There's No Business Like Show Business*.

I'm finding that sincerity and ~~trying~~ to be ~~as~~ simple or direct as possible (I'd like)
is often taken for sheer Stupidity
but since it is not a sincere
world - (it's very probable that being sincere is stupid)
One probably is stupid to
be sincere since its in this world
and know other world that we know
for sure we exist - meaning that -
(since reality exist it should be, must be dealt)
there is reality to deal with
since / should be ~~met~~ and delt with
with)

I'm ~~Sick~~ MM. - I'm not permitted ~~to~~
Edward R. Murrows show)

problems
nervousness
humanness
blunders
mistakes
and my own
thoughts

This of course is taken for over drinking -

(a few drinks
to many - occasionally)
meaning maybe I
didnt have time to
eat during day
and since socially
liquor is accepted
possibly precariously
and hurriedly - I might
feel a need to relax
with a few glasses of sherry
that might react quickly

That perhaps
I would have
not enjoyed
being ~~too~~ tired
and make
me suddenly
gay and respon-
sive to things
and people
around me

and the more I think of it
the more I realize there are no answers
life is to be lived

and since it is compairitively so short – (maybe to short – maybe to long – for sure) it isnt easy the only thing I know,

now that I want to live me notold and I feel sudenly not concerned about previous things except to protect myself my life – and to desperatly pray & tell the univers I trust it

fear

wonderment

the wondering of something ask it questions –

about not getting the D. out – after four days

the unbelievableness of the actually if it happened

or the pleading & promising of of anything – reasoning – which is more conventional.

slip in writing?

I started to write after Buddy

Bad instead of Buddy

with fear

Because A.I. punished me and whipped me – the bad part of my body she said – must never touch myself there or let any one – wash cloth – water dripping from it)

and the immediate fear of any part of my body there – fear to touch my own body

I'm finding that sincerity
and ~~trying~~ to be ~~as~~ simple or direct as (possible) I'd like
is often taken for sheer stupidity
but since it is not a sincere world—
it's very probable that being sincere is stupid.
One probably is stupid to
be sincere since it's in this world
and no other world that we know
for sure we exist—meaning that—
(since reality exists it ~~should be must be dealt~~ should be met and dealt with)
since there is reality to deal with

I'm ~~not~~ M.M.—I'm not permitted ~~to be~~
Edward R. Murrow's show

problems
nervousness
humanness
blunders
mistakes
and my own
thoughts

(a few drinks
too many—**occasionally**)
meaning maybe I
didn't have time to
eat during day
and since socially
liquor is accepted
and possibly previously
hurrying—I might
feel a need to relax
with a few glasses of sherry
that might react too quickly

that perhaps
I would have
not enjoyed
being too tired
and make
me suddenly
gay and respon-
sive to things
and people
around me

this of course
is taken for
over-drinking

and the more
I think of
it the more
I realize there
are no answers
life is to be
lived

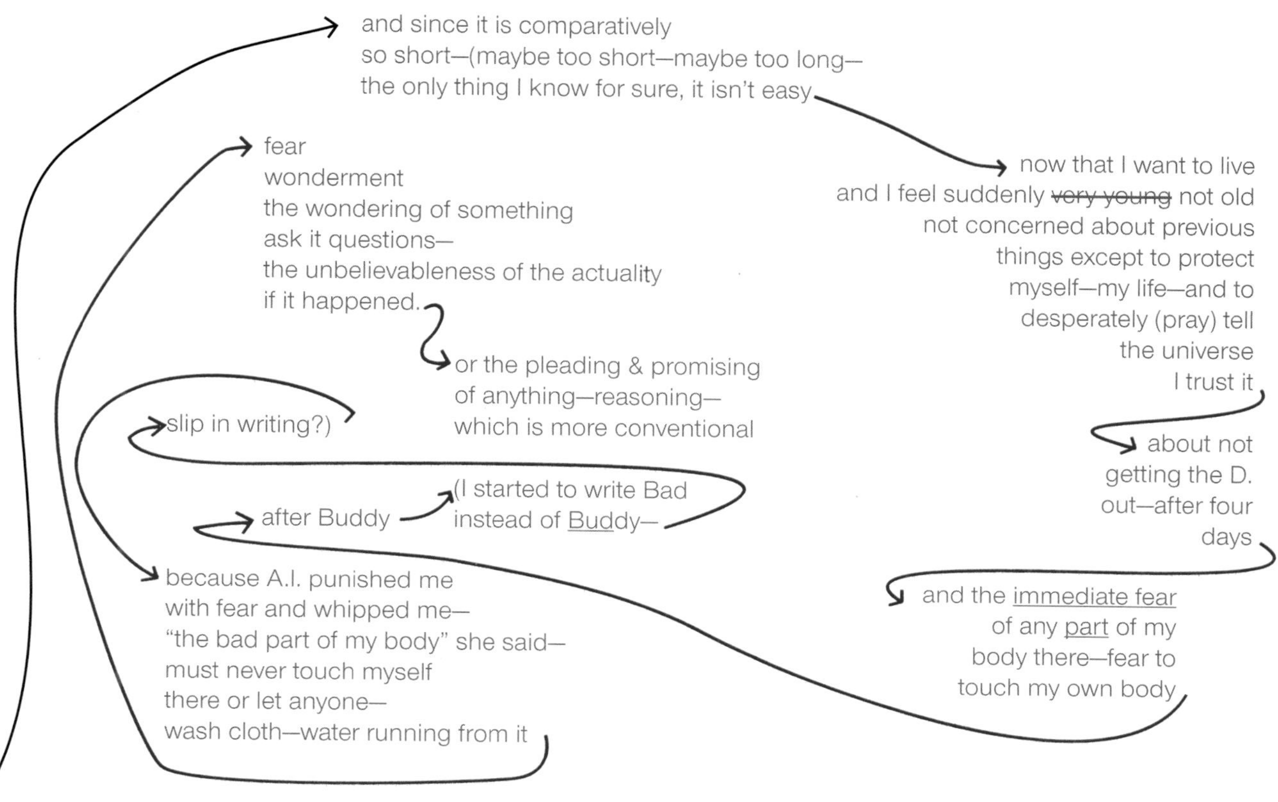

and since it is comparatively
so short—(maybe too short—maybe too long—
the only thing I know for sure, it isn't easy

now that I want to live
and I feel suddenly ~~very young~~ not old
not concerned about previous
things except to protect
myself—my life—and to
desperately (pray) tell
the universe
I trust it

about not
getting the D.
out—after four
days

and the immediate fear
of any part of my
body there—fear to
touch my own body

after Buddy

(I started to write Bad
instead of Buddy—

slip in writing?)

because A.I. punished me
with fear and whipped me—
"the bad part of my body" she said—
must never touch myself
there or let anyone—
wash cloth—water running from it

fear
wonderment
the wondering of something
ask it questions—
the unbelievableness of the actuality
if it happened.

or the pleading & promising
of anything—reasoning—
which is more conventional

Notes:
Marilyn was a guest on Edward R. Murrow's very popular TV show *Person to Person* on April 8, 1955.

A.I. was probably Aunt Ida, that is, Ida Martin, the other Aunt Ida (the first being Ida Bolender), a great-aunt with whom Marilyn lived from November 1937 to August 1938 in Compton, California.

In the spring of 1938, Marilyn may have suffered a sexual assault by one of her fellow boarders, who could be the Buddy mentioned here.

The "D." may be short for either "doctor" or "demon."

THE AMBOY DUKES
Big Brokers

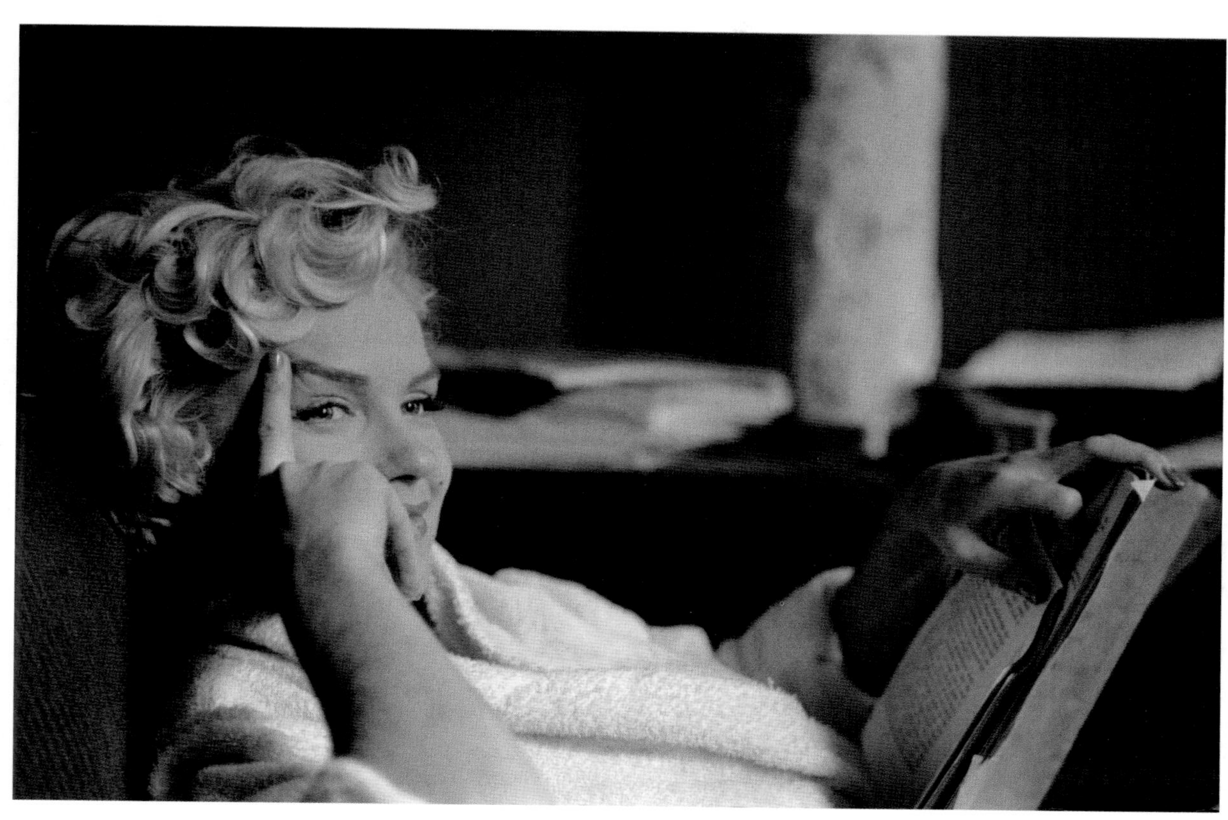

In a bookstore in Los Angeles, February 1953
On the set of *The Seven Year Itch*, 1954

PARKSIDE HOUSE STATIONERY

1956

Soon after their wedding on June 29, 1956, Marilyn and Arthur Miller went to London, where the film *The Prince and the Showgirl*, produced by Marilyn Monroe Productions, was to be shot. Laurence Olivier directed the film and played the male lead. The relationship between the two actors was difficult: Olivier was disdainful and haughty toward Marilyn.

The couple arrived in London on July 14 and stayed at Parkside House, a luxurious manor house in Egham, Surrey, near London. Everything should have been idyllic.

However, one day Marilyn found her husband's open diary and discovered that the playwright was disappointed in her, that he was sometimes ashamed of her in front of his intellectual peers, and that he had doubts about their marriage. Marilyn was extremely upset and felt betrayed.

Did she write these few poems and odd texts on Parkside House stationery before or after her discovery? In either case, their tone is mournful. They are pessimistic about love and love's possibilities as well as the inevitable passage of time.

The filming was difficult. Marilyn's acting coach Paula Strasberg was called in to help, as was Dr. Margaret Hohenberg, her New York analyst. On October 29, Marilyn Monroe was introduced to Queen Elizabeth II during a ceremony, and she went back to the United States on November 20.

The portrait on page 121 is possibly of Laurence Olivier.

PARKSIDE HOUSE,
ENGLEFIELD GREEN,
SURREY.
EGHAM 800.

my love sleeps besides me -
in the faint light - I see his ~~face~~ manly jaw
give ~~a~~way - and the mouth of his
boyhood returns
with a softnes softer
its sensitivness ~~that~~ trembling
in stillness
his eyes must have look out
wonderously from the cave of the little
boy - when the things he did not understand -
he forgot

---

but will he look like this when he's dead
oh unbearable fact inevitable
yet sooner would I rather his love die
than him?

my love sleeps besides me—
in the faint light—I see his manly jaw
give ~~a~~way—and the mouth of his
boyhood returns
with a softness softer
its sensitiveness ~~that~~ trembling
in stillness
his eyes must have look out
wonderously from the cave of the little
boy—when the things he did not understand—
he forgot
but will he look like this when he is dead
oh unbearable fact inevitable
yet sooner would I rather his love die
than/or him?

>>>

the pain of his longing when he looks
at another –
like an unfulfilment since the day
he was born.

and I in merciless pain
and with his pain of longing –
when he looks at and loves another
like an unfulfilment of ~~since~~ the day
he was born –
we must endure
I more sadly because I can feel no joy

>>>

the pain of his longing when he looks
at another—
like an unfulfillment since the day
he was born.

And I in merciless pain
and with his pain of Longing—
when he looks at and loves another
like an unfulfillment of ~~since~~ the day
he was born—
we must endure
I more sadly because I can feel no joy

PARKSIDE HOUSE,
ENGLEFIELD GREEN,
SURREY.
EGHAM 800.

(On) silence, ~~who~~ ~~don't~~ aren't ~~your~~ ~~soothe me~~ still,
you ~~drums~~ sounds stillness hurt my ~~ears~~ head - and
pierce ears with sounds unbearable - durable
Jars my head with the stillness of

on the screen of pitch blackness
reappears - Comes the shapes of monsters ~~who are~~
my most steadfast companions -

my blood ~~is~~ throbbing with unrest
turns it route in ~~the~~ one ~~opposite~~ others direction
and the ~~whole~~ world is asleeping
ah peace I need you - even a
peaceful monster.

>>>

oh silence ~~why don't/aren't you still soothe me~~
you ~~sounds drums~~ stillness hurt my ~~ears~~ head—and
pierce ears
jars my head with the stillness of
sounds unbearable/durable—
on the screen of pitch blackness
comes/reappears the shapes of monsters ~~who are~~
my most steadfast companions—
my blood ~~is~~ throbbing with unrest
turns it route in ~~the opposite~~ another direction
and the ~~whole~~ world is sleeping
ah peace I need you—even a
peaceful monster.

521 WISSELL

PARKSIDE HOUSE,
ENGLEFIELD GREEN,
SURREY.
EGHAM 800.

To have your heart is
the only ~~happy~~ proud (that ever belonged
to me) ~~thing~~ ~~possession~~ completly (posession ~~I've~~ ever
possessed So

Thing that ever complettly
happen to me

521 Wissett

To have your heart is
the only completely happy proud ~~possession~~ thing (that ever belonged
to me) I've ever possessed so

thing that ever completely
happen to me

Note: Wissett is a village in Suffolk. It is not known what the number refers to; possibly it is a phone number.

PARKSIDE HOUSE,
ENGLEFIELD GREEN,
SURREY.
EGHAM 800.

I guess I have always been
deeply
terrified ~~of~~ to really be some ones
wife
since I know from life
one cannot love another,
ever, really,

I guess I have always been
deeply terrified ~~at~~ to really be someone's
wife
  since I know from life
one cannot love another,
ever, really.

PARKSIDE HOUSE,
ENGLEFIELD GREEN,
SURREY.
EGHAM 800.

it is not to be for granted

that the old woman hides -

from her glass - the one she polishes so it won't be dusty - letting sometimes to

to see her toothless gasp and if perhaps she very gently smiles -

she remembers -

her pain

her pale chiton dress

that she wore on a windy afternoon when she walked

where noone had ever been

her clear eyed baby who

lived to die - The women years have

left - The woman stairs in space

it is not to be for granted
~~in life less that~~ the old woman hides—
from her ~~mirror~~ glass—the one she polishes so it won't be dusty—
daring sometimes ~~that to~~
to see her toothless gasp and if she perhaps very gently smiles
~~years only~~ she remembers—
her ~~life or imagined youth~~ pain
her pale chiffon dress
that she wore on a windy
afternoon when she walked
where no one had ever been
her ~~blue eyed~~ clear eyed baby who
lived to die—the woman's ~~youth~~ years have
~~not~~ left. The woman stares & stares in space

PARKSIDE HOUSE,
ENGLEFIELD GREEN,
SURREY.
EGHAM 800.

where his eyes rest with pleasure - I want to still be - but time has changed the hold of that glance -

alas how will I cope when I am even less youthful -

I seek joy but it is clothed with pain -

take heart ~~Have Courage - to be brave~~ as in my youth sleep and rest my heavy head on His breast - for ~~because~~ still my love sleeps beside me.

where his eyes rest with pleasure—I
want to still be—but time has changed
the hold of that glance.
    Alas how will I cope when I am
even less youthful—

I seek joy but ~~you are~~ it is clothed
with pain—
~~have courage—to be brave~~ take heart as in my youth
sleep and rest my heavy head
on ~~your~~ his breast—~~because~~ for still my love
sleeps beside me.

PARKSIDE HOUSE,
ENGLEFIELD GREEN,
SURREY.
EGHAM 800.

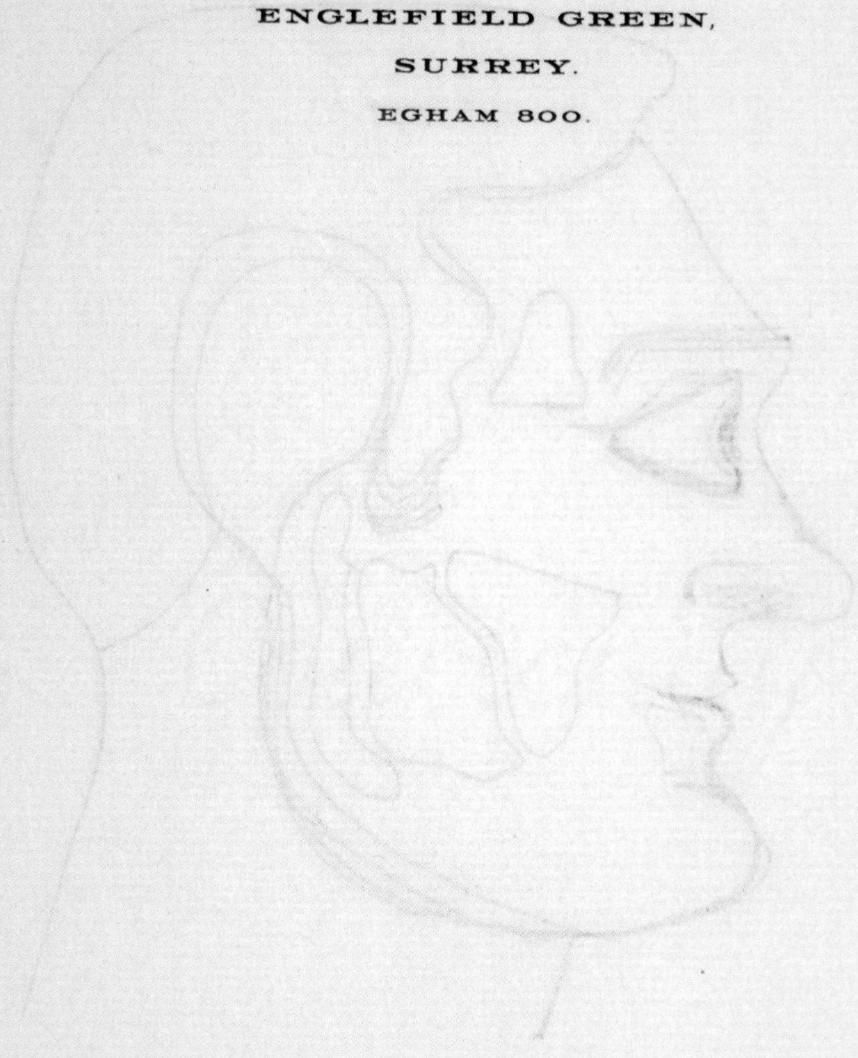

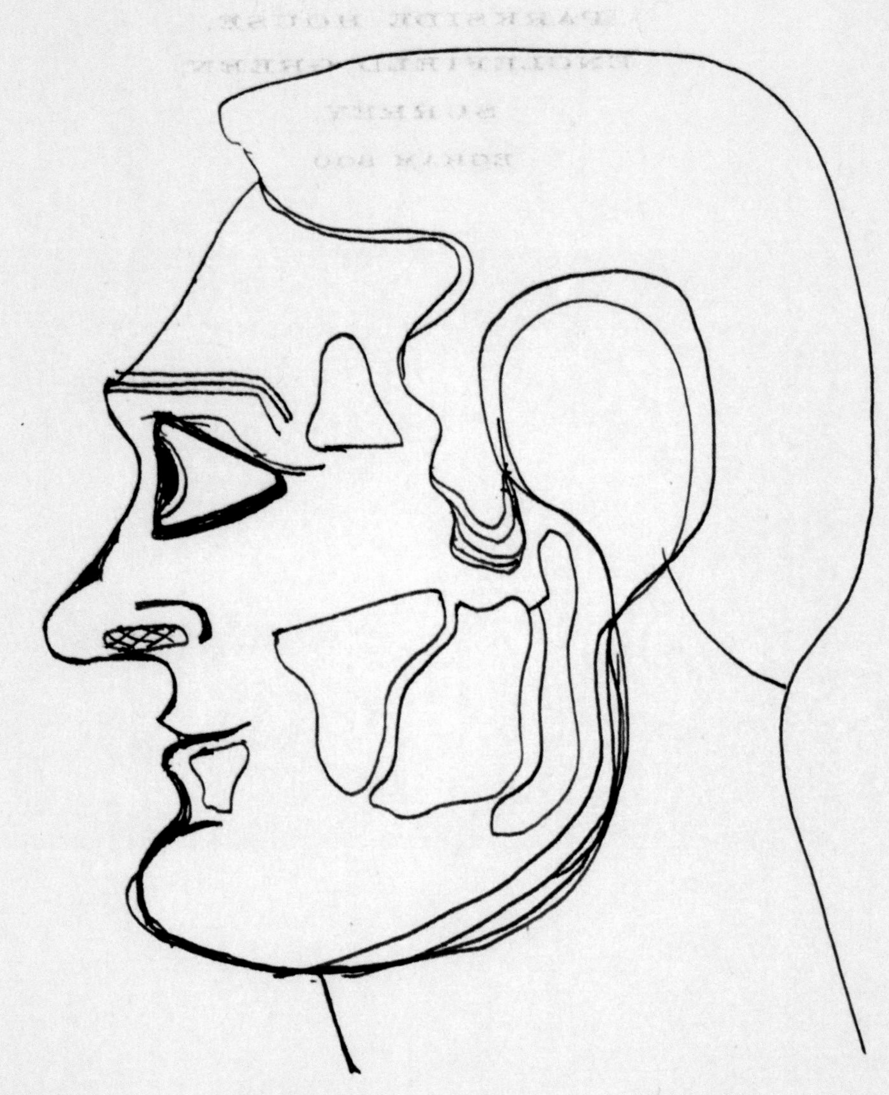

Marilyn reading Whitman's *Leaves of Grass*, 1951
Marilyn reading Arthur Miller's *Death of a Salesman*, 1952

DEATH OF A SALESMAN
PULITZER PRIZE
CRITICS CIRCLE AWARD
ANTOINETTE PERRY AWARD
THEATRE CLUB AWARD
FRONT PAGE AWARD
BY ARTHUR MILLER
THE IDEA OF A THEATER
DESIGNING FOR FILMS
The ART of ACTING
STAGE TO SCREEN
A History of the THEATRE
FREEDLEY and REEVES
CROWN
25 best PLAYS
BRITISH PLAYS
Television

ROXBURY NOTES

1958

In the summer of 1957, Marilyn and Arthur Miller bought a house in Roxbury, Connecticut, where Arthur had already lived with his first wife. They initially considered having the house demolished in order to have a new one built by Frank Lloyd Wright, with a swimming pool, a home cinema, a theater, and a big office for Arthur, but the project turned out to be too expensive and they contented themselves with renovating the property.

Marilyn probably wrote these few pages in the spring of 1958, and their tone is particularly disenchanted. The couple stayed a long time in the country, but, loveless now, their home seemed empty. Arthur worked with little success on the screen adaptation of his own short story *The Misfits*, and Marilyn quickly got bored with her role of housewife. Even the arrival of spring and leaves on the trees were no longer any solace, since they reminded her of failed attempts at motherhood, the lack of a child she had hoped for. At this time she would look closely at her own face in a magnifying glass and observe the effects of passing time.

Since the "other" (the beloved) was unattainable, she resigned herself "to love bravely" and accept what she could not alter. Here we can sense a tortured soul who still wanted to believe in the possibility of profound connection, even as the relationship grew more strained and distant.

starting tomorrow I will take
care of myself for that's
all I really have and as I
see it now have ever had.
Roxbury—I've tried to imagine
spring all winter—its here and
I still feel hopeless. I think
I hate it here because there
is no love here anymore. I
regret the effort I desperately made
here. I tried to fight what with
my being I knew was true
~~that~~ due to pressures, (as going to sound like a telegram) that have come
in my work (its funny I've always
accepted even the worst—tried to oppose it
if it meant jeopardizing my work)
he could not endure (he is not upset ...) changes I
felt (innocently, while I am ~~smart~~) that
what I could endure helped both
of us and in a material way ~~also~~ which
means so much more to him
than me ever.—I have seen
what he intends me to see and
I am strangely calm while I catch
my breath. Its a good saying—the not
so funny—what it stands for—(though) pain
"If I had my life to live over I'd
live over a salon" [Those tender green
~~leaves~~ on these one hundred & seventy five
year old maples that I see (~~[illegible]~~
~~[illegible]~~) (what my senses ~~[illegible]~~)—what was I looking at)—its like
having a child when one is ninety.
~~I don't want any children~~ because I only
~~could~~ ~~[illegible]~~ trust every ~~delicate and~~
~~indelicate feeling of~~ my child ~~with~~
~~myself~~ in case of accident (sounds like
~~an identification card.~~) There is no one
~~I trust.~~ I mean if anything would happen (blessed thought) at this moment. In early spring the green is
too sharp—though the delicacy in their form is

starting tomorrow I will take care of myself for that's all I really have and as I see it now have ever had. Roxbury—I've tried to imagine spring all winter—it's here and I still feel hopeless. I think I hate it here because there is no love here anymore. I regret the effort I desperately made here. I tried to fight what with my being I knew was true~~—that~~ due to pressure (it's going to sound like a telegram) that have come in my work (it's funny I've always accepted even the worst—tried to oppose it if it meant jeopardizing my work) he could not endure (he is from another land) though I felt (innocently, which I am <u>not</u>) that what I could endure helped both of us and in a material way ~~also~~ which means so much more to him than me even. I have seen what he intends me to see and I am strangely calm while I catch my breath. It's a good saying the not so funny—what it stands for though—pain "If I had my life to live over I'd live over a saloon"

Those tender green leaves on these one hundred & seventy five year old maples that I see (~~I wondered several what my senses felt~~ what was I looking at). It's like having a child when one is ninety. ~~I don't want any children because I only could trust every delicate and indelicate feeling of my child with myself in case of accident (sounds like an identification card)~~ there is no one I trust. I mean if anything would happen Blessed thought at this moment. In every spring the green is too sharp—though the delicacy in their form is

>>>

Note: The quote is from W. C. Fields.

sweet and uncertain ~~th~~ – it puts up a good struggle in the wind trembling ~~all~~ the while. Those leaves will relax, expand in the sun and each rain drop they will resist even when their battered and ripped.
I think I am very lonely – my mind jumps. I see myself in the mirror now, brow ~~furrowed~~ – if I lean close I'll see what I dont want to know – tension, sadness, disappointment, my ~~[illegible]~~ eyes dulled cheeks flushed with capilaries that look like rivers on maps – hair lying like snakes. the mouth makes me the saddest next to my dead eyes. there is a dark line between the lips in the outline of several brown waves in a turbulent storm – It says dont kiss me, dont fool me I'm a dancer who cannot dance

When one wants to stay alone as my love (arthur) indicates the other must stay apart

>>>

sweet and uncertain ~~though~~ it puts up a good struggle in the wind ~~though~~ trembling all the while. Those leaves will relax, expand in the sun and each raindrop they will resist even when they're battered and ripped. I think I am very lonely—my mind jumps. I see myself in the mirror now, brow furrowed—if I lean close I'll see—what I don't want to know—tension, sadness, disappointment, my ~~blue~~ eyes dulled, cheeks flushed with capillaries that look like rivers on maps—hair lying like snakes. The mouth makes me the saddest, next to my dead eyes. There is a dark line between the lips in the outline of several [illegible] waves in a turbulent storm—it says don't kiss me, don't fool me I'm a dancer who cannot dance.

When one wants to stay alone as my love (Arthur) indicates the other must stay apart.

>>>

re-relationships-

Everyones Childhood *plays* itself out

No wonder no one knows the other or can completely understand By this I don't know if I'm just giving up with this conclusion or resigning myself — or maybe for the first time connecting with reality -

how do we know the pain of anothers earlier years, let alone all that he drags with him since along the way at best a lot of lea-way is needed for the other — yet how *much* is *unhealthy* for one to bear

I think to love bravely is the best and accept — as much as one can bear

>>> re—relationships

Everyone's childhood plays itself out
No wonder no one knows the other or can completely understand.
By this I don't know if I'm just giving up with this conclusion or resigning myself—or maybe for the first time connecting with reality—

how do we know the pain of another's earlier years let alone
all that he drags with him since along the way at best a lot of lee-way is needed for the other—yet how much is unhealthy for one to bear.

I think to love bravely is the best and accept—as much as one can bear

THE IDIOT

Marilyn reading a script, Hotel Bel-Air, Los Angeles, 1952
Marilyn on her bed, Hollywood, 1962

livewire®

49¢ WIDE RULED NUMBER LW-49

RED LIVEWIRE NOTEBOOK

1958

In the spring of 1958, Marilyn had had enough of her dull country life. She wanted to start working again and was studying proposals from her agent and Fox, among which was an adaptation of Faulkner's *The Sound and the Fury,* when, out of the blue, Billy Wilder sent her a two-page summary of an old German farce he was working on, *Some Like It Hot*. On July 8 she arrived in Los Angeles for the shooting.

Marilyn used only five pages of this big red spiral notebook. It can be dated from the summer of 1958, as it includes two lines of dialogue from *Some Like It Hot* (pages 140 and 142). Why these two lines? (One might be self-referential; Marilyn was born in June just like the character of Sugar Kane.) What do they reveal about Marilyn's musings?

Another possibility presents itself: that the pencil notes were written before the ones in blue ballpoint pen. In that case, "after one year of analysis" (page 138) would refer to 1956 (she started her analysis with Dr. Hohenberg in 1955), with a hint of irony as to the result, as revealed in a short four-line poem expressing despair in the form of a cry for help: the desire to die rather than live.

I left my house of green rough wood
a blue velvet couch I dream till now
a shiny dark bush just left of the door.
I down the walk slickity clack as my doll
in her carriage went over the cracks "We'll
go far away"

look —
we left
We'll leave our outlines on the crushed grass the meadow as we reaching — they're touching the sky
It will die sooner because we were there — will something else never grow?
the blue and still white clouds changing by from an
old man shapes to a smiling dog with ears flying

Don't cry my doll don't cry
I hold you and rock you to sleep
hush hush I was only pretending now, I was
not your mother who died.

I shall feed you from the shiny dark bush
just left of the door

I left my home of green rough wood—
a blue velvet couch I dream till now
a shiny dark bush just left of the door.
~~[Illegible]~~ down the walk clickity clack as my doll
in her carriage went over the cracks—"We'll go far away"

The meadows are huge the earth (will be) hard
on my back. The grass ~~surged~~ touched
the blue and still white clouds changing from an
old man shapes to a smiling dog with ears flying

Look—
The meadows are reaching—they're touching the sky
~~We'll leave~~ We left our outlines against/on the crushed grass.
It will die sooner because we were there—will something
else have grown?

Don't cry my doll don't cry
I hold you and rock you to sleep.
hush hush ~~I'm~~ I was only pretending now ~~that~~ I'm (was)
not your mother who died.

I shall feed you from the shiny dark bush
just left of the door.

Jamaica 3/6/78

after one year of analysis

Dr. Mike Fayer

Help Help
Help
I feel life coming closer
when all I want -
is to die

Scream -
You began and ended in a[illegible]
but where was the middle?

Jamaica 36/78
Dr. Mike Fayer

After one year of analysis

Help Help
Help
I feel life coming closer
when I all want
is to die.

Scream—
You began and ended in air
but where was the middle?

Notes:
It has been impossible to trace Dr. Mike Fayer.

According to Donald Spoto, Marilyn is thought to have sent the five-line poem "Help" to Norman Rosten in the summer of 1961 after having started regular consultations with Dr. Ralph Greenson. Spoto adds that Marilyn first wrote this poem, or perhaps message, in Arthur Miller's notebook in London in 1956.

I'm not very bright I guess

No just dumb if I had any brains I wouldn't be on crummy train with this crummy girls band

I used to play with male bands but I can't afford it any more

Have you ever been with a male band

That

I'm not very bright I guess.

No just dumb//if I had
any brains I wouldn't be
on crummy train with this
crummy girls' band.

I used to sing with male
bands but I can't afford it
anymore.
Have you ever been with a male band

Heats

Note: This is a line from the scene in the train near the beginning of *Some Like It Hot*.

you know I'm going to be
twenty five in June

You know I'm going to be
twenty-five in June

Note: This is also a line from *Some Like It Hot*. When the film was made Marilyn had turned thirty-two, but her birthday was June 1.

Title - about my poems

Norman - so hard to please
when all I want is to tease
so it might ryme
so whats the crime?
after all this
~~when I've spent all this time~~
on earth

Title—About my poems.

Norman—so hard to please
when all I want is to tease
so it might rhyme
so what's the crime?
~~When I've spent all this~~ After all this time
on earth

Note: Norman Rosten, poet and novelist, had been a close friend of Marilyn's in New York since 1955.

Marilyn Monroe with Carson McCullers, during a lunch given by the American author in honor of the great Danish writer Karen Blixen (Isak Dinesen), at McCullers's home in Nyack, New York, 1959
Marilyn with Blixen and McCullers

FRAGMENTS AND NOTES

The notes and fragments written here and there—on torn-out pages, envelopes, tickets, address books—bring together secrets, observations, efforts at self-motivation and introspection. They also show Marilyn's will, which was bent sometimes on purely practical matters and at other times on the general question of self-discipline. Ways of interpreting one line or other, confusion at having to act a joyful part when she felt sad, the need to concentrate harder, birthday greetings with all kinds of fanciful names (she loved inventing nicknames for her friends or herself), memories of her mother wanting to keep her out of the way, rules for life and work, reminders for fittings for a gala evening dress, instructions for her business partner Milton Greene, and, at the beginning of an address book, a list of instructions to be followed: in each text we glimpse a moment of her life, a character trait, signs of doubt or uneasiness, and, over and over, the desire to improve and transform herself.

aug 21

I am restless and nervous and scattered and jumpy—
a few minutes ago I almost threw a silver plate—into a dark area on the set—but I knew couldn't afford to let out anything I really felt in fact I couldn't dare because I wouldn't stop at that maybe. just before that I almost threw up my whole lunch. I'm tired. I'm searching for a way to play this part I am depressed with my whole life since I first remember—How can I be such a gay young hopeful girl—what I am using is that one sunday when I was fourteen for I was all those things that day but—Why can't I use it more consistantly—my concentration wavers most of the time—something is racing in me in the opposite direction to most of the days I can remember. I must try to work and work on my concentration—maybe starting with the simplest of things—

Aug 27

I am restless and nervous and scattered and jumpy—a few minutes ago I almost threw a silver plate—into a dark area on the set—but I knew couldn't afford to let out anything I really felt in fact I wouldn't dare because I wouldn't stop at that maybe. Just before that I almost threw up my whole lunch. I'm tired. I'm searching for a way to play this part I am depressed with my whole life since I first remember—How can I be such a gay young hopeful girl—What I am using is that one sunday when I was fourteen for I was all these things that day but—Why can't I use it more consistently my concentration wavers most of the time—something is racing in me in the opposite direction to most of the days I can remember. I must try to work and work on my concentration—maybe starting with the simplest of things.

M.M.

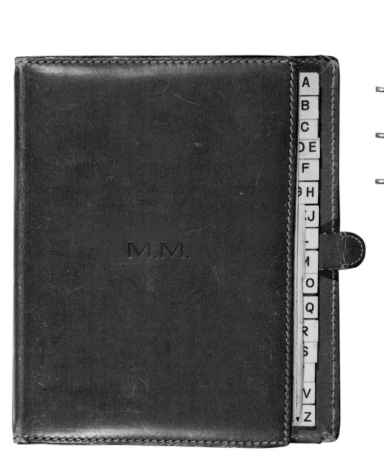

must have the discipline to Must make effort to do the following –

z – go to class – my own always – without fail

x – go as often as possible to observe Strassberg's other private classes

g – never miss actors studio sessions

v – work whenever possible – on class assignments – and always keep working on the acting exercises

u – start attending Clurman lectures – also Lee Strassberg's directors lectures at theater wing – enquire about both.

l – keep looking around me – only much more so – observing – but not only myself but others and everything – take things for what they are worth.

Y – must make strong effort to work on current problems and phobias that out of my past has arisen – making much much much more more more more more effort in my analisis. And be there always on time – no excuses for being ever late.

try to enjoy myself when I can – I'll be miserable enough as it is

w – If possible – take at least one class at University – in literature –

Firenze

Via della Vigna Nuova, 47

Milano

Via Monte Napoleone, 5

GUCCI

O – follow RCA thing through.

Roma

Via Condotti, 21

New York

7 East 58th Street at Fifth Avenue

P – try to find someone to take dancing from – body work (creative)

T – Take care of my instrument – personally & bodily exercise

Words – Find out their meanings

Wanderjahre – pertaining somehow to the word Entsagung – (what does that mean to)? does it mean sacrifice.

à trois does it mean like – probation

Must make effort to do
must have the discipline to do the following—
z - go to class—my own always—without fail
x - go as often as possible to observe Strasberg's other private classes
g - never miss my actors studio sessions
v - work whenever possible—on class assignments—and always keep working on the acting exercises.
u - start attending Clurman lectures—also Lee Strasberg's directors' lectures at theater wing—enquire about both
l - keep looking around me—only much more so—observing—but not only myself but others and everything—take things (it) for what they (it's) are worth.
y - must make strong effort to work on current problems and phobias that out of my past has arisen—making much much much more more more more more effort in my analysis. And be there always on time—no excuses for being ever late.
w - if possible take at least one class at university—in literature—
o - follow RCA thing through.
p - try to find someone to take dancing from—body work (creative)
t - take care of my instrument—personally & bodily (exercise)

try to enjoy myself when I can—I'll be miserable enough as it is.

Words—Find out their meanings

Wanderjahre—pertaining somehow to the word Entsagung—(what does that mean to)? does it mean sacrifice.

à trois does it mean like—probation

Notes:
The names in this address book, especially that of Milton Greene, would seem to indicate that it was bought in New York in 1955.

Harold Clurman, theater director and drama critic, was one of the three founders of Group Theatre in New York in 1931 (along with Lee Strasberg).

Marilyn Monroe signed a contract to record film songs with the RCA label in 1954.

There is no obvious link between "Wanderjahre" (the wandering years) and "Entsagung" (renunciation), unless Marilyn is echoing her reading of Freud or Rilke.

"À trois"/"threesome" bears at most a dubious connection with "probation."

12:00 Ceil Chapman –
530 7th Ave –
4th floor
tel # LA-4-5800

~~Saturday Morning 12:00 –~~

~~Sunday~~ Night Actors Benefit – at least dinner for them some where? ask

speak to Paula – about scenes for me in the future

Saturday Afternoon 2:30
Lee Strasberg Matenee
Cat on Hot tin Roof

Sat Morn – Profile time call about them Chapman

Monday Night
Hair – instead of Tues have done on Mon. morning – also ask about comb out for Mon Night
Dress –

Fri Night –
John Moore fitting

Fri Morning
8:30 – Franciscan Hair
11:00 Actors Studio

Call Milton about –

1 – a day a week with Hohenberg – Saturday – because leaving and need it and Wellesley
2 – about paying Hohenberg's Bill – which didn't give him yet (can we pay it on Mon?)
3 – about white shoes because probably wear white dress (what about wrap?)

Call Lois Weber & Jacobs about yesterday papers mainly Herald Tribune and times.

12:00 Ceil Chapman—
530 7th ave—
4th floor
tel # LA-4-5800

Saturday Morning 12:00
Sunday Night—Actors Benefit
dinner for them somewhere? At least ask
speak to Paula—about scenes for me in
the future

Monday Night
Hair—instead of tues. have done
on Mon. morning—also ask about
comb out for Mon. night.
Dress—
Saturday afternoon 2:30
Lee Strasberg matinee
Cat on a Hot Tin Roof
Sat Morn—Profile time call about then
C. Chapman

Fri Night
John Moore fitting

Fri Morning
8:30—Francis [illegible] Hair
11:00 Actors Studio

Call Milton about—
1—6 days a week with Hohenberg—
Saturdays—because learning and need
it and she willing
2—about paying Hohenbergs—
Bill—which didn't give him
yet—(can we pay it on Mon?)
3—about white shoes because probably
wear white dress
(what about wrap?)

Call Lois Weber or A. Jacobs
about all yesterday's papers
mainly Herald Trib and Times

Notes:
This note was probably written in December 1955, as the Actors Studio benefit party was held in New York on December 12, to which, however, Marilyn wore a black dress (see photo on page 192).

Paula Strasberg, Lee Strasberg's wife, was also a very close friend and became Marilyn's coach during film shoots.

Ceil Chapman has often been said to have been Marilyn's favorite fashion designer.

John Moore, couturier and interior designer, decorated the Millers' apartment at 444 East 57th Street in 1955. He created several dresses for Marilyn, including the wedding dress she wore when she married Arthur Miller.

Arthur Jacobs, who was head of his own company, took care of public relations for Marilyn from 1955 until her death.

Lois Weber, who worked for the Arthur P. Jacobs Company, was Marilyn's press agent in New York.

For Kris
Sept 9

James 10th Birthday on TV
same year

– Remember, Somehow how Mother always tried to get me to "go out" as though she felt I were too unadventurous. She wanted me even to show a cruelty toward women. I this in my teens. In return, I showed her that I was faithful to her.

For Kris
Sept. 9

Jane's 12th birthday on 7th
same year

—Remember, somehow, how—
Mother always tried to
get me to "go out" as
though she felt I
were too unadventurous.
She wanted me even
to show a cruelty
toward woman. This
in my teens. In return,
I showed her that I
was faithful to her.

Notes:
Kris was undoubtedly Dr. Marianne Kris, Marilyn's New York analyst from 1956 to February 1961.

Jane Miller, Arthur's elder daughter, was born on September 7, 1944; therefore, this note must have been written in 1956.

For Life

It is rather a determination not to be overwhelmed.

For Work

The truth can only be recalled, never invented

for life
It is rather a determination not to be overwhelmed.

for work
The truth can only be recalled, never invented

forgive us for being sentimental

if only

Hope this finds you feeling just great – no that's not what I want to say – I mean – forgive me

You've got style – the way you've moved along these years –

Slow me up

Mate
Late
Rate –
ate

for being sentimental

I'm so glad you were born and that I'm living at the same time as you –

Love (we all love you)

Noodle
Sam
Max
Clump
Scagw finny
pussy
and all the rest
of us –

I mean

Forgive us for being sentimental
if only

Hope this finds you feeling
just great—no that's not what
I want to say [~~illegible~~]—I mean—forgive me

for being sentimental
I'm so glad you were born
and that I'm ~~alive~~ living at the
same time as you.

You've got style—the way you've
moved along these years.
Slow me up
Mate
Late
Rate
ate

~~Happy Birthday~~ Love (we all love you)
Noodle
~~no I mean I mean~~ Sam
Max
Clump
Sugar Finny
Pussy
and all the rest
of us . . .

Note: This short prose piece and the variation on it on the following page were very likely written on the occasion of Norman Rosten's birthday. "She gave herself pretty names. One day, she signed a note with Noodle, Sam, Max, Clump, Sugar Finny, Pussy, and so on. An identity name, the little funny imp. It was a very attractive aspect of her personality: she had a great sense of humor" (Norman Rosten, *Marilyn Among Friends*).

it's time for
statement
Amen for statements
we feel

intrumental
sentimental
merely incidental
coincidental

not a tear you'll see
forgive me if I'm

influence by tender feeling
affecting the emotions

Senamental.
meaning – influenced by tender
feelings

ourselves or myself
Sense

Sensable – sensitive

Happy Birthday (we all love you)
Sam
Max
Champ
Sugar Fanny
Pussy
and all the rest
of us –

It's time for
sentiment
I know how sentimental we feel

instrumental
sentimental
merely incidental
coincidental

Not a tear you'll see
Forgive me if I'm

influence by tender feelings
affecting the emotions
meaning—sentimental ~~is a~~ influenced for
tender
feelings
ourselves or myself

sense

sensible—sensitive

Happy birthday and love (we all love you)
Noodle
Sam
Max
Clump
Sugar Finny
Pussy
and all the rest of us—

Hurts dream –
262
263
Feb 28

Dec 11
See in older journal –
Always admired men who had many women
It must be that to a child of a dissatisfied woman the idea of monogomy is hallow –

Starts dream—
262
263
Feb 28

Dec 11
See in older journal—
always admired men who had many women.
It must be that to a child of a dissatisfied woman
the idea of monogamy is hollow

Note: The numbers 262 and 263 probably refer to the same collection of song standards as those on page 82 (the Waldorf-Astoria series). The titles these correspond to are "While We're Young" (262) and "Wonderful Guy" (263).

pardon me - I'm sorry to wake you
But I wonder if you could help
me

I'm being abducted

you know kiddnapped - by him

I thought maybe as soon as
we got some place I'd ask the
driver to stop and let me off
But we been driving for hours
and we still don't seem to be
noryhere at all - not only that
but I'm freezing to death - I
aint got ~~[illegible]~~ nothin on under
my coat

Pardon me—I'm sorry to wake you
But I wonder if you could help
me

I'm being abducted

you know—kidnapped—by him

I thought maybe as soon as
we got some place I'd ask the
driver to stop and let me off
But we been driving for hours
and we still don't seem to be
nowhere at all—not only that
but I'm freezing to death—I
ain't got much on under
my coat

sleeping prince - for paula

learn-lines lodgically

don't stop Myself

- I can't do more Than one thing at a time

Name tasks - 1-2-3 etc

Make map tonight

T - weariness

Take my time to Think -

Write out part - copying

Work on exercises

1 - Cold

Sleeping prince—for Paula

don't stop myself
Name tasks—1 - 2 - 3 - 4 etc.

T—weariness

write out part—copying it

work on exercises
1—cold

learn—lines logically

—I can't do more than
one thing at a time
make map tonight

take my time to think—

Note: *The Sleeping Prince* was the first title for *The Prince and the Showgirl*, which was filmed in London in 1956. This note must have been written the same year.

He said that
I've become deified
as a sex symbol
That
public never except me as
a virgin and as a ~~Twee~~ nineteen year old turning

he wants ~~to~~ discovers
~~feel~~ he
and he alone is ~~to~~
responsible

reality
is better

Eli

9 — his lose.

tennesse — wants me

tells Eli—
new ending

I don't want anybody else

He said that
I've become so deified
as a sex symbol
that public never **accept** me as
a virgin and as a nineteen/twenty year old

he wants to
feel he discovers reality
and he alone is is better
responsible

Eli
g—his lose
tennesse**e**—wants me

tells Eli—
new ending

I don't want anybody else

Note: Marilyn wanted to play the title role in Elia Kazan's 1956 film *Baby Doll*, written by Tennessee Williams and starring Eli Wallach. However, Carroll Baker got the part.

I feel the camera has got to look through Gays eyes whenever he is in a scene and even when he is not - there still have the a sense of him

He is the center and the rest move around him

but I guess Houston will see to that

he is both subtle and overt in his leading them and (in his cruelity and his tenderness (when he reaches out of himself for her - R.)

I feel the camera has got
to look through Gay's
eyes whenever he is in a
scene and even when he is
not there still has to be a sense of
him
He is the center and the
rest move <u>around</u> him
but I guess Houston will
see to that
He is both subtle and
overt in his leading them
and in his cruelty and his tenderness
(when he reaches out of himself
for her—R.)

Notes:
John Huston's (here spelled "Houston") film *The Misfits* was shot in Nevada, in the summer of 1960. Arthur Miller adapted the script from his own short story, the role of Roslyn having been inspired by his wife. The atmosphere was extremely tense, especially between the couple, whose marriage was foundering. Marilyn, a perfectionist, was frequently late—very late—frightened of not being ready for the challenge, and often groggy from the barbiturates she had begun to depend on. She was awestruck to be acting with Clark Gable, who was a lifelong idol and whom she had sometimes thought of, or dreamed of, as her own father. Marilyn had already been directed by John Huston in *The Asphalt Jungle*, the film that, in spite of a minor role, had put her name in lights. In a sense, in *The Misfits* she acted out her own life with a disquieting and magnificent closeness that must have been enormously tormenting.

It is likely that this note was written during the first half of the shooting, in July. Gay (Langland) is the name of the character played by Clark Gable. The final "R" refers to Roslyn (Taber), Marilyn's character.

Marilyn at Costello's restaurant, New York, 1955

KITCHEN NOTES

1955 or 1956

Contrary to the image we may have of Marilyn as often disorderly and chaotic, she attended to some aspects of daily life with care and even meticulousness. When she had to decorate an apartment or house she made notes, took measurements, collected samples or patterns, and decided on color schemes and the arrangement of furniture. Similarly, when she organized a dinner for Helen Schneider's birthday, very likely at the end of 1955 in New York, she wrote a long, exacting list of everything she had to prepare or check out. Each detail was planned, down to the table decorations and bathroom requisites. This party may have taken place when Marilyn moved into an apartment on the corner of Sutton Place and 57th Street after her long stay in a suite at the Waldorf-Astoria, which had turned out to be too costly for Marilyn Monroe Productions.

Incidentally, Marilyn sometimes enjoyed cooking, and when she did she noted recipes down to the last ingredient, step by step, including the quality of produce needed.

ask for kitty + or clyde

my white dishes - all of them - from West-port

my old silver candle holders

my paintings two - big dutch women Angels an drunken

get fire wood - what about silverware -

buy - white toilet seat

buy - hamper or good thing for bathroom for towels, tables etc. & or thing for back of door

buy - lamps for bedroom also shades take Kirt with me -

buy foot stool & coffee table (ask M. morromulyan)

~~buy ... ...~~ at L & taylors

buy two chairs classic for in front of piano also serves for extra guest chairs

buy brass ash trays one for M - one for Le - one for me

buy chandliers - one for hall - one for dinning table take back the two glass silver things

buy twelve linnin napkins - silver ware - for 12

buy birthday present for Helen -

have Kirt paint places for chandleirs also where railing broke

have Milton & Kirt put pictures in hallway - help me arrange room - & place

have - Kirt saw off legs of Candle Holders

dry clean - comforter

have wash - bathroom rugs

send out laundry

call - ~~piano~~ tuner

paintings 2

coffee table

Bergdorf

Barr

ask for Kitty & or Clyde
my white dishes—all of them from Westport
my old silver candle holders
my paintings two—dutch woman big one and drunken angels
get firewood—what about silverware
buy—white toilet seat
buy—hamper & or gold thing for bathroom & or thing for back of door
for towels, bottles, etc

buy—lamps for bedroom—also shades take Kirt with me
buy foot stool & coffee table (ask M. Moumulion)
buy bar buy mirror at L. & Taylors
buy two chairs—classic—for in front of piano, also serves for extra guest chairs
buy brass ash trays one for M. one for L. one for me
buy chandeliers—one for hall—one for dining area—take back the two glass silver things
buy twelve linen napkins—silverware—for 12
buy birthday present for Helen—

have Kirt paint places for chandeliers also where railing broke
have Milton & Kirt put pictures in hallway—help me arrange room & place
have Kirt saw off legs of brass candle holders

dry clean comforter
have wash—bathroom rugs
send out laundry

call Moumulion
guest towels
paintings 2

coffee table
[indecipherable] glass bar

Notes:
Kitty and Clyde may have provided Marilyn with occasional help.

Kirt seems to have been a man who did odd jobs for Marilyn.

M. Moumulion: unidentified.

The reference to Milton Greene would mean this birthday dinner took place between 1955 and 1956. Marilyn stayed at Milton and Amy Greene's property in Westport, Connecticut, when she first arrived on the East Coast and often visited them in subsequent months.

champane? | at least some kind of wine with dinner

buy - liquor - Scotch - Gin - Vermouth

Ordores - Cavier - others?

two roasts - 1 - prime ribs of beef 1 - turkey

Have Hedda make dressing / with endive hearts

large mixed green salad - avacado? (Also aspick?

not done too well

vetables - Frozen peas or in pod? - kitty squash? or something

Potatoes - of some kind - ? ask kitty

Celery hearts - olives - ~~scallions~~? - Radishes

ask Hedda about

Fruit & Ice cream for dessert - choc. & vanilla

Coffee & cookies & danish pastery for later

Birthday Cake for Helen -

Geo. Leslie & me 2

Hedda & Norman 2

Elliott & Sessie 2

~~Helen & Isadore~~ 2

George Brasilla & wife 2

Guy & friend with guitar 2

Murry hill - 2 5409

French prov. white 2 sizes

Marble top coffee table

Buy for less than he says

LLOYDS

Bloomingdales

wine glass 1/2

Linen Napkins

or more

towels

Ivory Flakes or Snow

Rinso Blue or detergent

champagne? at least some kind of wine with dinner
buy—liquor—scotch—gin—vermouth—
hors d'œuvres—caviar—others?

two roasts— 1—prime ribs of beef 1—turkey
have Hedda make dressing
large mixed green salad with endive hearts—avocado? (Also aspic?)
vegetables—frozen peas or in pod?—not done too well—Kitty's squash? or something
Potatoes—of some kind—? ask Kitty
Celery hearts—olives—scallions?—Radishes
ask Hedda about fruit & ice cream for dessert—choc & vanilla
Coffee & cookies & danish pastry for later
Birthday cake for Helen—
Geo. Leslie & me 2
Hedda & Norman 2
Ettore & Jessie 2
Helen & Isadore 2
George Brusilla [Braziller] & wife 2
Guy & friend with guitar 2

Murray Hill—25400
french prov. white
marble top 2 sizes
coffee table
buy for less than he says
Lloyds 116 E 60th

Bloomingdales?
Wine glasses 12
linen napkins
6 or more guest towels

Ivory. Flakes or snow
Rinso Blue or detergent

Notes:
Geo. Leslie: unidentified.

Isadore Schneider (1896–1976) was born in the Ukraine and emigrated with his family to the United States in 1904. A novelist and critic, he was a friend of Norman Rosten's, knew Arthur Miller, and worked as a reader for George Braziller at Grove Press. Helene Berlin Schneider was his wife.

Ettore Rella (1907–1988) was a poet and playwright. His wife was named Jessie.

George Braziller was born in 1916 and founded his own publishing house in 1955. His wife was Marsha.

Guy: unidentified.

CITY TITLE INSURANCE COMPANY

68 SUTTER STREET Phone GArfield 1-8530

"Complete Title and Escrow Service"

No garlic

sourdough French bread - soak in cold water for chicken wring out then shed

giblets - boil in water - 5-10 min liver + heart then chop

1 whole or ½ onion - chop & parsarly four stalk celery chop together

following spices - put in rosemarie thyme - bay leaf - oregano - poultry season salt - pepper - Grated cheese (parmisan) - 1 handful

½ lb. - ¼ lb Ground round - put in frying pan - brown (no oil) then mix

rasian 1½ cups or more

walnuts
chestnuts } 1 cup chop nuts
pinuts

1 or 2 hard boiled eggs - chopped

mix together | salt & pepper in side chicken or turkey - outside same w/ butter

no garlic
sourdough
french bread—soak in cold water wring out
then shred

for chicken giblets—boil in water—5–10 min.
liver heart then chop

1 whole or ½ onion—chop & parsley four stalk celery chop together
following spices—put in rosemary
thyme—bay leaf—oregano—poultry seasoning—salt—pepper—
grated Parmesan cheese—1 handful
½ lb.—¼ lb ground round—put in frying pan—brown (no oil) then mix
raisin 1½ cups or more
walnuts
chestnuts { 1 cup chop nuts
peanuts

1 or 2 hard boiled eggs—chopped
mix together

salt & pepper inside chicken

or turkey—outside same and butter

>>>

Sew up or clamp birds
put Chicken or turkey in 350° Oven

Roasting Chicken - 3 or 4 lbs. or larger
cooks 30 min to 1. lbs.

Vinegar

oil
onion
spices

brown Chicken or phesant

let cook in own juice

add little water as you go

1/2 glass Vinigar - put in when half don

cooks 2 hours.

put potatoes

mushroom - button canned

peas - fresh

>>>

sew up or clamp birds
put chicken or turkey in 350° oven
roasting chicken—3 or 4 lbs. or larger
cooks 30 min to 1 lbs.

Vinegar
oil
onion
spices

brown chicken
or pheasant

let cook in own juice
add little water as you go
½ glass vinegar—put in when half done
cooks 2 hours
put potatoes
mushroom—button canned
peas—fresh

LEE AND PAULA STRASBERG

When Marilyn arrived in New York at the beginning of 1955, she soon found her heart's dream: the Actors Studio, which she hoped would open the doors to a new status as an artist. Just as quickly, Lee Strasberg saw how exceptional she was, bursting with a talent seeking to express itself fully. However, Marilyn had a major shortcoming: she was always late. Lee had his reservations about this, and when she admitted that she was absolutely unable to be on time, he replied cuttingly: "Well, be early then." This explains the playful tone of the brief text in which she quotes a line from one of her early films that speaks of punctuation instead of punctuality . . .

The fragile confidence she developed often shifted to anguish and despair. What would happen if she lost her concentration, the only thing that kept an actor from suicide, to repeat Lee Strasberg's striking phrase?

In February 1961, Marilyn thought she was checking into the hospital for a rest cure but instead found herself confined to a psychiatric cell at Payne Whitney in New York. Her friends couldn't respond to her cry for help, as, legally speaking, they weren't family members (Joe DiMaggio, whom she had divorced in 1954, would finally rescue her from this nightmare). In any case, Marilyn proved single-minded. Prompted by her sense of having escaped from quicksand, in a resolute letter to Lee Strasberg dated December 19, 1961, she laid out her plan for a new independent production company, which would make sense to her only if Lee were associated with it. To the very end, she wanted to be free of the studios, but this time she wanted to challenge them on their turf, in Hollywood.

oh
yes Mr Oxley is always
complaining about my punctuation
so I'm careful to get here
before 9:00 Mr. Oxley is on
telephone won't you sit down

loose – letting go
voice starts back there

Don't be nervous Marilyn
you are doing swell &
you look wonderful –
L.

Oh yes Mr. Oxley is always
complaining about my punctuation
so ~~now~~ I'm careful to get here
before 9:00. Mr. Oxley is on
telephone won't you sit down

loose letting go
voice starts back theatre

[following is written by Lee Strasberg]
Don't be nervous Marilyn
you are doing swell &
you look wonderful—
L.

Notes:
The chronically late pupil used this line from *Monkey Business* (the 1952 Howard Hawks film in which Mr. Oxley is Marilyn's director) with no little humor when addressing her teacher (who may have been speaking on the telephone at that moment).

To judge by his reply, it is not clear that Lee Strasberg understood either the allusion or the quotation.

Dear Lee

One of the most personally helpful things I've heard so far in my life was what you said in class friday afternoon - It was helpful ~~in That I feel as though I'm a little bit~~ freeer - ~~also more - I can't Think of any t mean by that~~ More ~~relaxed~~ 2 and 2 dont ~~necessarily make~~ 4.

Dear Lee

One of the most personally helpful things I've heard so far in my life was what you said in class friday afternoon—it was helpful ~~in that I feel as though I'm a little bit freer—also more—I can't think of any I mean by that more relaxed~~ 2 and 2 don't necessarly make 4.

Paula dear,
you asked me yesterday
why—

I felt somehow (I'm only
conscious of it this morning)
that if I didn't have the
control or the will to make
myself do anything or complete & do it right I
would never ~~a~~ be able
to get or do anything— I know
it sounds crazy— maybe
it was even superstitious
I don't know— I don't know
anything

Something has happened
I think to make me lose
my confidence. I don't know
what it is.

All I know is I want
to __work__

Oh paula I wish I knew
why I am so anguished.
I think maybe I am crazy
like all the other members
of my family were, when I
was sick I was sure I was.

I'm so glad you are __with__ me here!

Paula dear,

You asked me yesterday why—

I felt somehow (I'm only conceiving of it this morning) that if I didn't have the control or the will to make myself do anything simple & do it right I would never be able to act or do anything—I know it sounds crazy—maybe it was even superstitious—I don't know—I don't know anything.

Something has happened I think to make me lose my confidence. I don't know what it is. All I know is I want to *work*.

Oh Paula I wish I knew why I am so anguished. I think maybe I'm crazy like all the other members of my family were, when I was sick I was sure I was. I'm so glad you are *with* me here!

Marilyn Monroe with Paula and Lee Strasberg, New York, 1955

Hotel Bel-Air

701 Stone Canyon Road, Los Angeles 24

Dear Lee,

I'm embarrised to start this, but thank you for understanding and having changed my life - even though you changed it I still am lost - I mean I can't get myself together - I think its because everything is pulling against my concentration - everything one does or lives is impossible almost.

You once said, the first time I heard you talk at the actors studio that "there is <u>only concentration</u> between the actor and suiside." As soon as I walk into a scene I lose my mental relaxation for some reason, - which is my concentration. My will is weak but I can't stand anything. I sound crazy but I think I'm going crazy.

Thanks for letting Paula help me on the picture she is the only really warm woman I've known. Its just that I get before camera and my concentration and everything I'm trying to learn leaves me. Then I feel like I'm not existing in the human race at all.

Love,

Marilyn

Note: It is very likely that this letter was written at the beginning of 1956, during the filming of Joseph Logan's *Bus Stop*, when Paula Strasberg worked as Marilyn's coach for the first time.

Dear Lee & Paula,

Dr Kris has had me put into the New York Hospital - psychiatric division under the care of two idiot doctors. they both should not be my doctors.

You havn't heard from me because I'm locked up with all these poor nutty people. I'm sure to end up a nut if I stay in this nightmare - please help me Lee, this is the last place I should be - maybe if you called Dr. Kris and assured her of my sensitivity and that I must get back to class so I'll be better prepared for "rain"

over

Lee, I try to remember what you said once in class that "art goes far beyond science"

And the scary memories around me I'd like to forget - like screaming woman etc.

please help me - if Dr Kris assures you I am all right - you can assure her I am not. I do not belong here!

I love you both.

Marilyn

P.S. forgive the spelling - and theres nothing to write on here I'm on the dangerous floor !! its like a cell can you imagine - cement blocks they put me in here because they lied to me about calling my doctor & Joe and they had the bathroom door locked so I broke the glass and outside of that I haven't done anything that is uncooperative

Dear Lee & Paula,

Dr. Kris has had me put into the New York Hospital—psychiatric division under the care of two <u>idiot</u> doctors—they <u>both should not be my doctors</u>.

You haven't heard from me because I'm locked up with all these poor nutty people. I'm sure to end up a nut if I stay in this nightmare—please help me Lee, this is the <u>last</u> place I should be—maybe if you called Dr. Kris and assured her of my sensitivity and that I must get back to class so I'll be better prepared for "Rain."

Lee, I try to remember what you said once in class "that art goes far beyond science."

And the scary memories around me I'd like to forget—like screaming woman etc.

Please help me—if Dr. Kris assures you I am all right—you can assure her <u>I am not</u>. I do not belong here!

I love you both.

Marilyn

P.S. forgive the spelling—and there is nothing to write on here. I'm on the dangerous floor!! It's like a cell can you imagine—cement blocks. They put me in here because they lied to me about calling my doctor & Joe and they had the bathroom door locked so I broke the glass and outside of that I haven't done anything that is uncooperative

Note: *Rain*, adapted from a Somerset Maugham short story, was a TV project that Lee Strasberg hoped to direct. Marilyn Monroe and John Gielgud were to have had the main parts. The film was never made because of a disagreement between NBC and Lee Strasberg.

December 19, 1961

Mr. Lee Strasberg
135 Central Park West
New York 23, New York

Dear Lee:

This is an important personal letter and please don't start to read it until you have the time to give it your careful thought. This letter concerns my future plans and therefore concerns yours as well since my future development as an artist is based on our working together. All this is an introduction; let me outline the recent events, my ideas and my suggestions.

As you know, for years I have been struggling to find some emotional security with little success, for many different reasons. Only in the last several months, as you detected, do I seem to have made a modest beginning. It is true that my treatment with Dr. Greenson has had its ups and downs, as you know. However, my overall progress is such that I have hopes of finally establishing a piece of ground for myself to stand on, instead of the quicksand I have always been in. But Dr. Greenson agrees with you, that for me to live decently and productively, I must work! And work means not merely performing professionally, but to study and truly devote myself. My work is the only trustworthy hope I have. And here, Lee, is where you come in. To me, work and Lee Strasberg are synonymous. I do not want to be presumptuous in expecting you to come out here for me alone. I have contacted Marlon on this subject and he seems to be quite interested, despite the fact that he is in the process of finishing a movie. I shall talk with him more thoroughly in a day or two.

Furthermore, and this must be kept confidential for the time being, my attorneys and I are planning to set up and independent production unit, in which we have envisaged an important position for you. This is still in the formative phase, but I am thinking of you in some consultative position or in whatever way you might see fit. I know you will want enough freedom to pursue your teaching and any other private interests you might want to follow.

Though I am committed to my analysis, as painful as it is, I cannot definitively decide, until I hear from you, because without working with you only half of me is functioning. Therefore, I must know under what conditions you might consider coming out here and even settling here.

I know this might sound quite fantastic, but if you add up all the possible advantages it should be a quite rewarding venture. I mean not only for Marlon and me -- but for others. This independent production unit will also be making pictures without me -- this is even required for legal reasons. This will offer an opportunity for Susan if she should be interested and perhaps even for Johnny. And Paula would have a great many opportunities for coaching. As for you, Lee, I still have the dream of you some day directing me in a film! I know this is a big step to take, but I have the wish that you might realize out here some of the incomplete hopes that were perhaps not fulfilled for you, like Lincoln Center, etc.

So I don't know how else to persuade you. I need you to study with and I am not alone in this. I want to do everything in my power to get you to come out -- within reason -- as long as it is to your advantage as well as mine. So, Lee, please think this over carefully; this is an awfully important time of my life and since you mentioned on the phone that you too felt things were unsettled, I have dared to hope.

I have meetings set up with Marlon and also with my attorneys and will phone you if there are any important new developments. Otherwise, please get in touch with me.

My love to all of you,

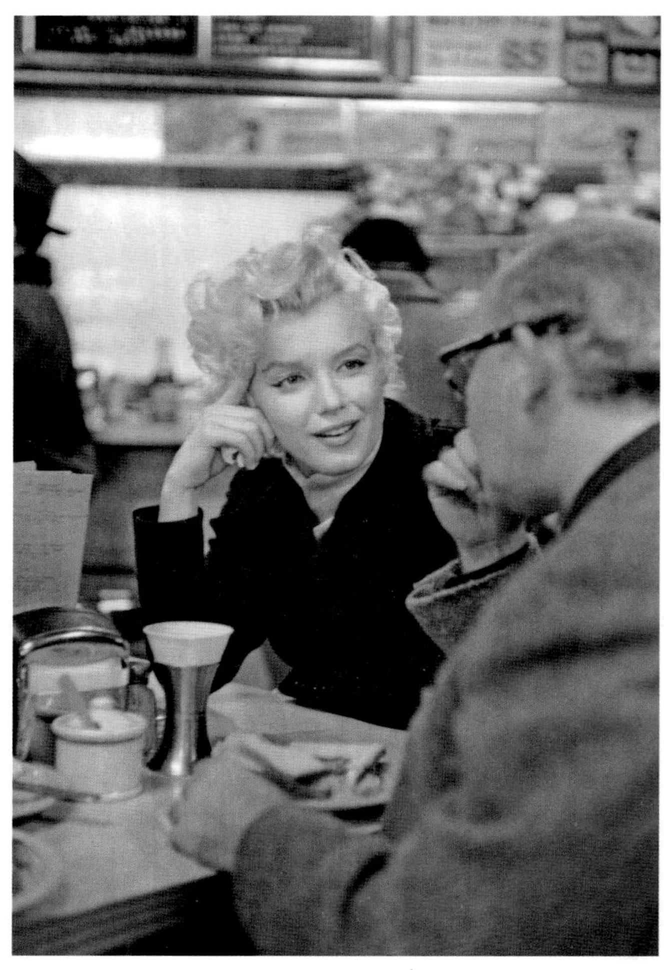

Marilyn Monroe and Lee Strasberg in a café
near Carnegie Hall in New York

LETTER TO DR. HOHENBERG

1956

Before accepting Marilyn as a student of his "Method," Lee Strasberg made it a condition that she start psychoanalysis. From the spring of 1955, therefore, three to five times a week, the actress consulted Dr. Margaret Hohenberg at 155 East 93rd Street in New York. Margaret Hohenberg was born in 1898 in Slovakia and had studied in Vienna, Budapest, and Prague before having to flee Austria in 1938 after the Anschluss. She first went to London for a year, then settled in New York in 1939.

Milton Greene, one of Dr. Hohenberg's patients, recommended her to Marilyn, and, curiously, the doctor accepted her as an analysand in spite of the obvious risk involved in treating two patients who not only knew each other but also had very close professional links. In fact, shortly after Milton Greene was fired from Marilyn Monroe Productions, the actress stopped seeing the analyst and never returned to her consulting rooms.

Nevertheless, a bill for $840, drawn up by Dr. Hohenberg on August 1, 1962, indicates that Marilyn had gotten back in touch with her former analyst for telephone consultations.

Dear Dr Hohenberg

I've been wondering myself why I don't write to you I've been feeling I was taken away from you (what your concern) or that you sent me away from you —

On the whole, things are going along rather well so far

M.C.A. our agents, and Shein, our lawyer, have been dealing with Natasha but — we'll see —

I have a strange feeling about Paula I mean — she works differently than Lee

Any way I keep feeling I won't be

but she is a wonderful and warm person — which also bewilders me able to do the part when I have too it like a horrible nightmare

Also I guess I didn't write you before this because I was waiting to see if I would get shot — first.

Arthur writes me every day — at least it gives me air to breathe — I can't get use to the fact that he loves me and I keep waiting for him to stop loving me though I hope he never will — but I keep telling myself — Who knows?

Dear Dr. Hohenberg,

I've been wondering myself why I don't write to you. ~~I think it has to do with the fact that~~ I've been feeling I was taken away from you (with your consent) or that you sent me away from you—

On the whole, things are going along rather well so far

M.C.A., our agents, and Stein, our lawyer ~~are dealing~~ have dealt with Natasha but—we'll see—

I have a strange feeling about Paula. I mean—she works differently than Lee but she is a wonderful and warm person—which also bewilders me

Anyway I keep feeling I won't be able to do the part when I have to it's like a horrible nightmare.

Also I guess I didn't write you before this because I was waiting to see if I would get shot first.

Arthur writes me every day—at least it gives me ~~a little~~ air to breathe—I can't get used to the fact that he loves me and I keep waiting for him to stop loving me—though I hope he never will—but I keep telling myself—who knows?

Notes:

In January 1953, Marilyn left the William Morris Agency, whose vice president, Johnny Hyde, had died in 1950. She signed a contract with the powerful talent agency MCA, Inc. (Music Corporation of America). George Chasin attended to Marilyn's interests at MCA until her death. In her book *Marilyn and Me*, Susan Strasberg quotes a story dating back to 1962 as told by Marilyn's masseur, Ralph Roberts: "She asked me if I had heard any rumors about Bobby Kennedy and herself. None of it is true, she told me. Besides, he is too skinny. Bobby is trying to dismantle MCA and has asked me to help him." Indeed, MCA had to wind down its agency work and concentrate on production after an action brought against the corporation by Attorney General Robert Kennedy in July 1962.

Irving Stein, along with Frank Delaney, was one of the lawyers who worked for Marilyn Monroe Productions.

In 1948, Natasha Lytess was appointed by Columbia, as was their usual practice, to help Marilyn prepare for her part in the Phil Karlson film *Ladies of the Chorus*. The two women worked together on about twenty films until Marilyn chose Paula Strasberg to assist her during the shooting of *Bus Stop* in February 1956. Natasha Lytess found it difficult to accept this break.

LETTER TO DR. GREENSON

1961

From January 1960 onward, following the advice of Marianne Kris (her analyst in New York at that time), Marilyn started analysis with Dr. Ralph Greenson in Los Angeles. She wrote him a long letter on March 2 and 3, 1961, about three weeks after her disastrous confinement at Payne Whitney, when she had had to confront one of her worst fears: the specter of hereditary family madness, the fear of ending up in a psychiatric hospital like her mother and grandmother before her.

At the time, Marilyn had been transferred from Payne Whitney after Joe DiMaggio's intercession and was convalescing at Columbia University's Presbyterian Medical Center. She was reading Freud, especially his letters. Bed-bound, she wrote describing the details of her confinement and all the misunderstandings that had led to her being placed in isolation. We can imagine her distress as she faced the guardians of normalcy whom she felt were ready to condemn her irrevocably. We are almost surprised at the moderate tone she used when discussing Dr. Kris's involvement, and the sense of perspective she had when recalling a scene in *Don't Bother to Knock* (directed by Roy Baker in 1952) that inspired her rebellion against the commitment and her (sham) suicide threat. We can find, too, in this poignant letter, the characteristic way Marilyn would suddenly change the subject to something positive in order to put her fears to one side: here her reconciliation with Joe DiMaggio, which had happened at Christmas.

Dear Dr. Greenson,

I'm having May Reis type this because it's not very clearly written, but I have also included these notes and you will see what I mean.

M.M.

March 2, 1961

Note: May Reis was Marilyn's personal assistant from the mid-1950s onward.

March 1,1961

Just now when I looked out the hospital window where the snow had covered everything suddenly everything is kind of a muted green. The grass, shabby evergreen bushes -- though the trees give me a little hope -- the desolate bare branches promising maybe there will be spring and maybe they promise hope.

Did you see "The Misfits" yet? In one sequence you can perhaps see how bare and strange a tree can be for me. I don't know if it comes across that way for sure on the screen -- I don't like some of the selections in the takes they used. As I started to write this letter about four quiet tears had fallen. I don't know quite why.

Last night I was awake all night again. Sometimes I wonder what the night time is for. It almost doesn't exist for me -- it all seems like one long, long horrible day. Anyway, I thought I'd try to be constructive about it and started to read the letters of Sigmund Freud. When I first opened the book I saw the picture of Freud inside opposite the title page and I burst into tears -- he looked very depressed (which must have been taken near the end of his life) that he died a disappointed man -- but Dr. Kris said he had much physical pain which I had known from the Jones book -- but I know this too to be so but still I trust my instincts because I see a sad disappointment in his gentle face. The book reveals (though I am not sure anyone's love-letters should be published) that he wasn't a stiff! I mean his gentle, sad humor and even a striving was eternal in him. I haven't gotten very far yet because at the same time I'm reading Sean O'Casey's first autobiography --(did I ever tell you how once he wrote a poem to me?) This book disturbs me very much in a way one should be disturbed for these things --after all,

There was no empathy at Payne-Whitney -- it had a very bad effect -- they asked me after putting me in a "cell" (I mean cement blocks and all) for <u>very disturbed</u> depressed patients(except I felt I was in some kind of prison for a crime I hadn't comitted. The inhumanity there I found archaic. They asked me why I wasn't happy there (everything was under lock and key; things like electric lights, dresser draws, bathrooms, closets, bars concealed on the windows -- the doors have windows so patients can be visible all the time, also, the violence and markings still remain on the walls from former patients). I answered: "Well, I'd have to be nuts if I like it here" then there screaming women in their cells -- I mean they screamed out when life was unbearable I guess -- at times like this I felt an available psychiatrist should have talked to them. Perhaps to alleviate even temporarily their misery and pain. I think they (the doctors) might learn something even -- but all are only interested in something from the books they studied -- I was surprised because they already knew that! Maybe from some live suffering human being maybe they could discover more -- I had the feeling they looked more for discipline and that they let their patients go after the patients have "given up". They asked me to mingle with the patients, to go out to O.T. (Occupational Therapy). I said: "And do what?" They said: "You could sew or play checkers, even cards and maybe knit". I tried to explain the day I did that they would have a nut on their hands. These things were furthest from my mind. They asked me why I felt I was "different" (from the other patients, I guess) so I decided if they were really that stupid I must give them a very simple answer so I said: "I just am".

The first day I did "mingle" with a patient. She asked me why I looked so sad and suggested I could call a friend and perhaps not be so lonely. I told her that they had told me that there wasn't a phone on that floor. Speaking of floors, they are all locked -- no one could go in and no one could go out. She looked shocked and shaken and said "I'll take you to the phone" -- while I waited in line for my turn for the use of the phone I observed a guard (since he had on a gray knit uniform) as I approached the phone he straight-armed the phone and said very sternly: "You can't use the phone". By the way, they pride themselves in having a home-like atmosphere. I asked them (the doctors) how they figured that. They answered: "Well, on the sixth floor we have wall-to-wall carpeting and modern furniture" to which I replied: "Well, that any good interior decorator could provide -- providing there are the funds for it" but since they are dealing with human beings why couldn't they perceive even an interior of a human being".

The girl that told me about the phone seemed such a pathetic and vague creature. She told me after the straight-arming "I didn't know they would do that". Then she said "I'm here because of my mental condition -- I have cut my throat several times and slashed my wrists" --she said either three or four times.

I just thought of a jingle:

"Mingle - but not if you
were just born single"

Oh, well, men are climbing to the moon but they don't seem interested in the beating human heart. Still one can change but won't -- by the way, that was the original theme of THE MISFITS -- no one even caught that part of it. Partly because, I guess, the changes in the script and some of the distortions in the direction and .....

LATER WRITTEN

I know I will never be happy but I know I can be gay! Remember I told you Kazan said I was the gayest girl he ever knew and believe me he has known many. But he loved me for one year and once rocked me to sleep one night when I was in great anguish. He also suggested that I go into analysis and later wanted me to work with his teacher, Lee Strasberg.

Was it Milton who wrote: "The happy ones were never born"? I know at least two psychiatrists who are looking for a more positive approach.

THIS MORNING, MARCH 2

I didn't sleep again last night. I forgot to tell you something yesterday. When they put me into the first room on the sixth floor I was not told it was a Psychiatric floor. Dr. Kris said she was coming the next day. The nurse came in (after the doctor, a psychiatrist) had given me a physical examination including examining the breast for lumps. I took exception to this but not violently only explaining that the medical doctor who had put me there, a stupid man named Dr. Lipkin had already done a complete physical less than thirty days before. But when the nurse came in I noticed there was no way of buzzing or reaching for a light to call the nurse. I asked why this was and some other things and she said this is a psychiatric floor. After she went out I got dressed and then was when the girl in the hall told me about the phone. I was waiting at the elevator door which looks like all other doors with a door-knob except it doesn't have any numbers (you see they left them out). After the girl spoke with me and told me about what she had done to herself I went back into my room knowing they had lied to me about the telephone and I sat on the bed trying to figure if I was given this situation in an acting improvisation what whuld I do. So I figured, it's a squeaky wheel that gets the grease. I admit it was a loud squeak but I got the idea from a movie I made once called "Don't Bother to Knock". I picked up a light-weight chair and slammed it, and it was hard to do because I had never broken anything in my life -- against the glass intentionally. It took a lot of banging to get even a small piece of glass - so I went over with the glass concealed in my hand and sat quietly on the bed waiting for them to come in. They did, and I said to them "if you are going to treat me like a nut I'll act like a nut". I admit the next thing is corny but I really did it in the movie except it was with a razor blade. I indicated if they didn't let me out I would harm myself -- the furthest thing from my mind at that moment since you know Dr. Greenson I'm an actress and would never intentionally mark or mar myself, I'm just that vain. Remember when I tried to do away with myself I did it very carefully with ten seconal and ten tuonal and swallowed them with relief (that's how I felt at the time.) I didn't cooperate with them in any way because I couldn't believe in what they were doing. They asked me to go quietly and I refused to move staying on the bed so they picked me up by all fours, two hefty men and two hefty women and carried me up to the seventh floor in the elevator. I must say at least they had the decency to carry me face down. You know at least it wasn't face up. I just wept quietly all the way there and then was put in the cell I told you about and that ox of a woman one of those hefty ones said: "Take a bath". I told her I had just taken one one the sixth floor. She said very starnly: "As soon as you change floors you have to take another bath". The man who runs that place, a high-school principal type, although Dr. Kris refers to him as an "administrator" he was actually permitted to talk to me, questioning me somewhat like an analyst. He told me I was a very, very sick girl and had been a very, very sick girl for many years. He looks down on his patients because I'll tell you why in a moment. He asked me how I could possibly work when I was depressed. He wondered if that interfered with my work. He was being very firm and definite in the way he said it. He actually stated it more than he questioned me so I replied: "Didn't he think that perhaps Greta Garbo and Charlie Chaplin perhaps and perhaps Ingrid Bergman they had been depressed when they worked sometimes but I said it's like saying a ball player like DiMaggio if he could hit ball when he was depressed. Pretty silly.

By the way, I have some good news, sort of, since I guess I helped, he claims I did. Joe said I saved his life by sending him to a psycho-therapist; Dr. Kris says he is a very brilliant man, the doctor. Joe said he pulled himself up by his own bootstraps after the divorce but he told me also that if he had been me he would have divorced him too. Christmas night he sent a forest-full of poinsettias. I asked who they were from since it was such a surprise,(my friend Pat Newcomb was there)-- they had just arrived then. She said: "I don't know the card just says "best, Joe". Then I replied: "Well, there's just one Joe". Because it was Christmas night I called him up and asked him why he had sent me the flowers. He said first of all because I thought you would call me to thank me and then he said, besides who in the hell else do you have in the world. He said I know I was married to you and was never bothered or saw any in-law. Anyway, he asked me to have a drink some time with him. I said I knew he didn't drink -- he said he now ocasionally takes a drink -- to which I replied then it would have to be a very, very dark place. He asked me what I was doing Christmas night. I said nothing, I'm here with a friend. Then he asked me to come over and I was glad he was coming though I must say I was bleary and depressed but somehow still glad he was coming over.

I think I had better stop because you have other things to do but thanks for listening for a while.

Marilyn M.

PS: Someone when I mentioned his name you used to frown with your moustache and look up at the ceiling. Guess who? He has been (secretly) a very tender friend. I know you won't believe this but you must trust me with my instincts. It was sort of a fling on the wing. I had never done that before but now I have - but he is very unselfish in bed.

From Yves I have heard nothing - but I don't mind since I have such a strong, tender, wonderful memory.

I am almost weeping.....

Marilyn with Edith Sitwell, London, 1956
Marilyn with Carl Sandburg, Los Angeles, 1961

WRITTEN ANSWERS TO AN INTERVIEW

1962

Whereas Marilyn often established bonds of trust and complicity with photographers, she was much more on her guard with journalists. That was why she prepared for interviews and often insisted on seeing the questions beforehand. That was obviously the case here, where we can read short draft answers she wrote to about thirty questions (the first few are missing) to give herself a lead. She invoked the master-pupil aspect of her relationship with Arthur Miller, and her difficulty in being a member of a group. No wonder that among the people she admired we find Eleanor Roosevelt (who was to die soon after Marilyn in November 1962), who was famous for her early feminism and opposition to racism, and who headed the U.N. commission to draw up the Universal Declaration of Human Rights. No less surprising was Marilyn's support for the Kennedy brothers, for their strength and youth and idealism. She also looked up to Carl Sandburg for his poetry, so sympathetic to the common man, as well as Greta Garbo, the other myth. A horrified vision of the H-bomb, support for all manner of persecuted people, a considered defense of psychoanalysis: the glamorous blonde was certainly no reactionary.

From her reference to Payne Whitney (where she had been confined for five days in February 1961) and from the books that the photographer George Barris, one of the last to shoot her, states she was reading a few days before her death, we may judge that these notes were written in 1962.

6 - Although this may be true in my estimation of an formal educational is never a basic cause for a material problem - it is the emotional background which matters

7 - (1) There was a pupil teacher relationship at the beginning of the marriage and but there was much more to the marriage than that (2) learned a great deal from it.

(3) A good marriage is a very delegate balance of many forces.

10 - experiences with any group of people is disalousing one has to discriminate the different members of a group. I never been very good at being a member of any group - more than a group of two that is.

payne whitney gives me a pain

11 - I was obviously an error of judgment to place me in payne whit. and the doctor who recomened realized it and tried to rectify it. what the my condition unwranted was the rest and care I got presbyterian Hospital

6 – although this may be true in my estimation of a formal education~~al~~ is <u>never</u> a basic cause for a material problem—it is the emotional background which matters

7 – (1) there was a pupil teacher relationship at the beginning of the marriage and ~~when~~ (2) I learned a great deal from it—a good marriage is a very delicate balance of many forces (3) but there was much more to the marriage than that

10 – experiences with any group of people is [illegible]
one has to discriminate the different members of a group. I never been very good at being a member of any group—more than a group of two that is.

11 – Payne Whitney gives me a pain
It was ~~often~~ obviously an error of judgment to place me in Payne Whit. and the doctor who recommended ~~it~~ realized it and tried to rectify it. What ~~the~~ my condition warranted was the rest and care I got at Presbyterian Hospital

12 the giving of myself work ~~and~~ a few reliable human beings the hope* for my future growth & development.

13 I have a strong sense of self of critacism but I believe I'm becoming more reasonable and tolerant realistic in this regard

(14-) Eleanor Roosevelt - her devotion to mankind
Carl Sandberg - ~~His poems~~ are songs of the people by the people and for people
Pres and Robert Kenedy - they symbolizes the youth of America - in its vigor its brilliance and its compassion
Greta Garbo - for her artistic creativity and her personal courage and integraty

(15) I am at ease with people I trust or admire or like the rest I'm not at ease with.

(16) - At the present time I'm reading Capt Newman M.D. and to kill a mocking bird - in times of crisis I do not turn to a book - I try to think and to use my understanding

(17) - I love poetry and poets

(18) I constantly try to clarify and redefine my goals

12 – the love of my work ~~I love~~ and a few reliable human beings
the hope for my future growth & development.

13 – I have a strong sense of self of criticism but I believe I'm becoming more reasonable and tolerant **realistic** in this regard

14 – Eleanor Roosevelt—her devotion to mankind
Carl Sandburg—his poems are songs of the people by the people and for people
Pres. and Robert Kennedy—they symbolize the youth of America—in its vigor its brilliance and its compassion
Greta Garbo—for her artistic creativity and her personal courage and integrity

15 – I am at ease with people I trust or admire or like the rest I'm not at ease with.

16 – At the present time I'm reading Capt. Newman M.D. and To Kill a Mockingbird—in times of crisis I do not turn to a book—I try to think and to use my understanding

17 – I love poetry and poets

18 – I constantly try to clarify and redefine my goals

Notes:
Captain Newman, M.D. is a novel by Leo Rosten (no relation to Norman), published in 1961, based on the experiences of Ralph Greenson when he was a military officer at Yuma (Arizona) during the Second World War. *To Kill a Mockingbird*, the Pulitzer Prize–winning novel by Harper Lee, was published in 1960.

In *Marilyn: Her Life in Her Own Words*, the photographer George Barris describes the conversation he had with her on August 3, 1962, the day before her death, when she told him she was reading these two books.

19 my sleep depends on my state of satisfaction and that varies with my life - my dreams are too intimate to be revealed in public. my nightmare is the H Bomb. whats yours?

20 ② But I have ~~not~~ always refrain from answering ~~~~ personal & religious questions

① I have great feeling for all the persecuted ones in the world.

21.- I hope at some future time to be able to make a glowing report about the wonders that psychoanalysis can achieve. The time is not ripe.

22 early lack of sufficient training and experience ~~~~

23- I would not wish to slight all the actresses who would be left off such a list and therefore refrain from answering

24- The lack of any consistant love and caring. a mistrust and fear of the world was the result. There were no benefits except what it could teach me about the basic needs of the young, ~~the sick~~ the sick and the weak.

25 I can't answer at this time

26 yes and I would underline it,

27 - in spades!

19 – my sleep depends on my state of satisfaction and that varies with my life—my dreams are too intimate to be revealed in public.
My nightmare is the H Bomb. What's yours?

20 – (1) I have great feeling for all the persecuted ones in the world
(2) But I ~~must~~ have always refrained from ~~discussing~~ answering personal religious questions.

21 – I hope at some future time to be able to make a glowing report about the wonders that psychoanalysis can achieve. The time is not ripe.

22 – Early lack of sufficient training and experience ~~as of yet until now~~

23 – I would not wish to slight all the actresses who would be left off such a list and therefore refrain from answering

24 – The lack of any consistent love and caring. A mistrust and fear of the world was the result. There were no benefits except what it could teach me about the basic needs of the young, the sick, and the weak.

25 – I can't answer at this time

26 – yes and I would underline it

27 – in spades!

SUPPLEMENTS

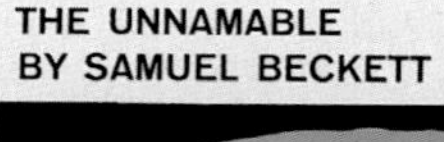

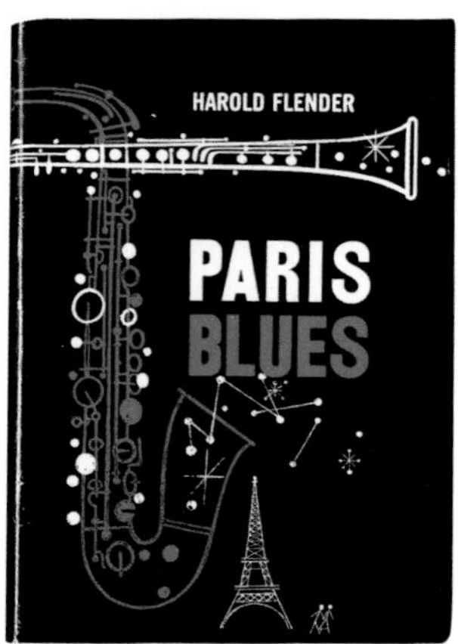

SOME BOOKS FROM MARILYN MONROE'S PERSONAL LIBRARY

Marilyn Monroe's library demonstrates her range of interests. Besides classics such as John Milton, Gustave Flaubert, Walt Whitman, James Joyce, and Khalil Gibran, she read widely from contemporary authors such as John Steinbeck, Ernest Hemingway, Samuel Beckett, Albert Camus, and Jack Kerouac.

The proceeds from the sale of Marilyn's books were donated by Anna Strasberg to the charity Literacy Partners. This was a logical choice, given Marilyn's love of books and reading, as well as Lee Strasberg's lifelong dedication to education.

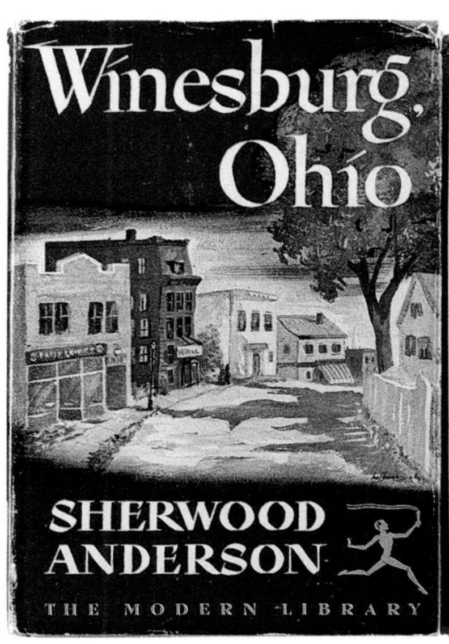
Winesburg, Ohio
SHERWOOD ANDERSON
THE MODERN LIBRARY

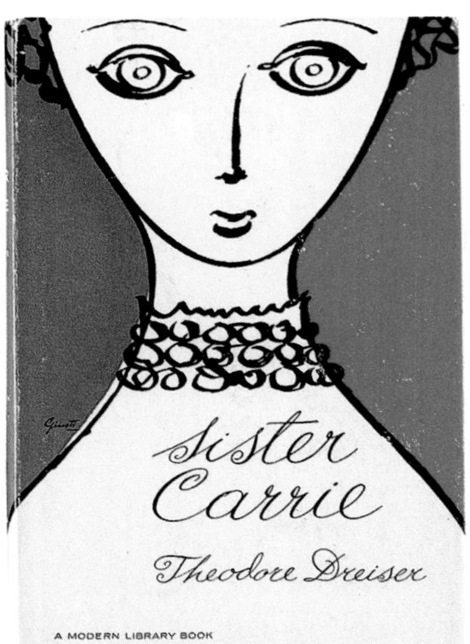
Sister Carrie
Theodore Dreiser
A MODERN LIBRARY BOOK

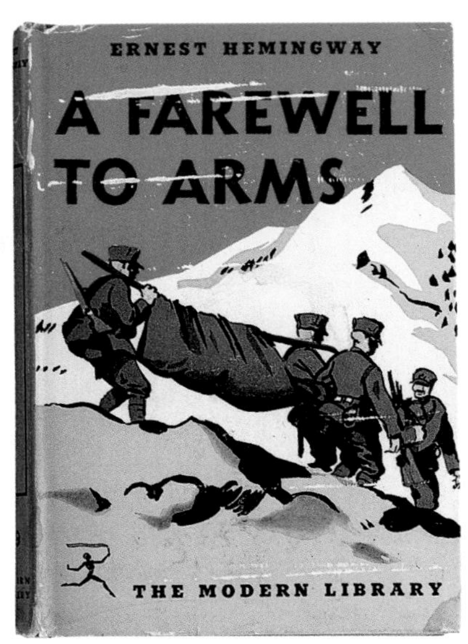
ERNEST HEMINGWAY
A FAREWELL TO ARMS
THE MODERN LIBRARY

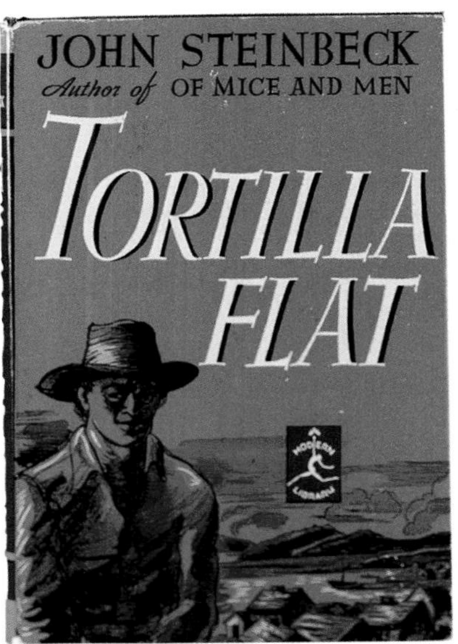
JOHN STEINBECK
Author of OF MICE AND MEN
TORTILLA FLAT

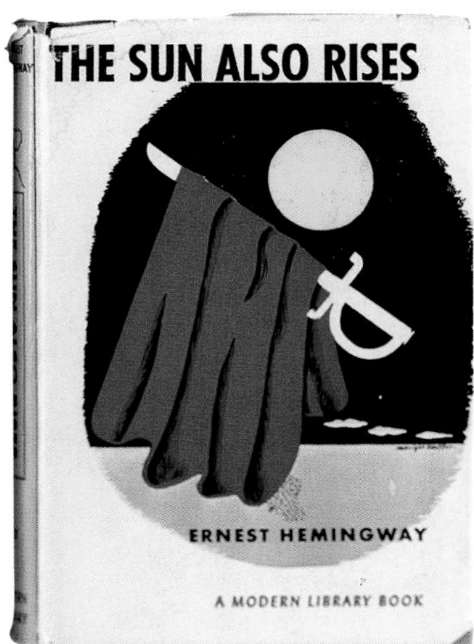
THE SUN ALSO RISES
ERNEST HEMINGWAY
A MODERN LIBRARY BOOK

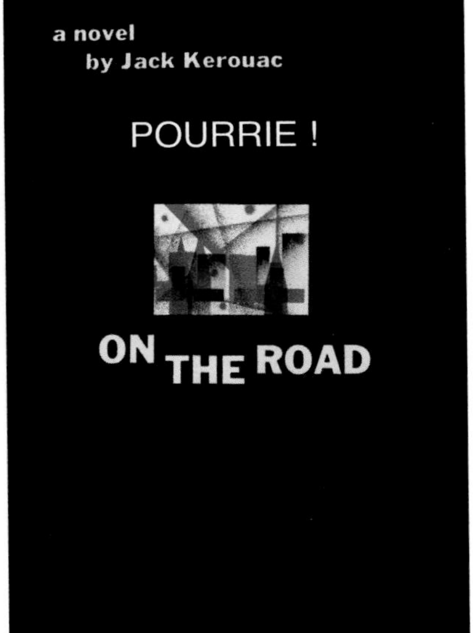
a novel
by Jack Kerouac
POURRIE !
ON THE ROAD

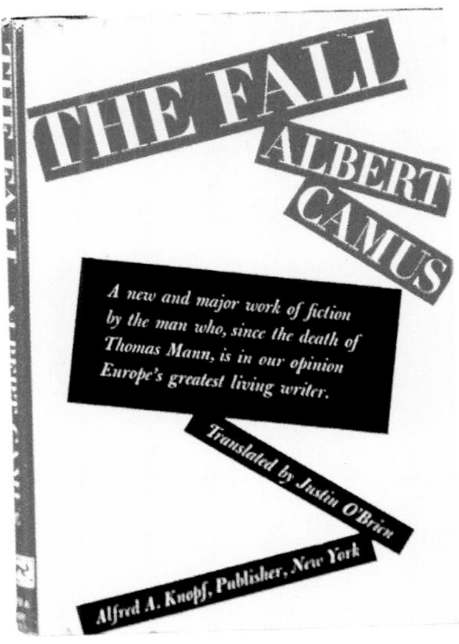
THE FALL
ALBERT CAMUS
A new and major work of fiction by the man who, since the death of Thomas Mann, is in our opinion Europe's greatest living writer.
Translated by Justin O'Brien
Alfred A. Knopf, Publisher, New York

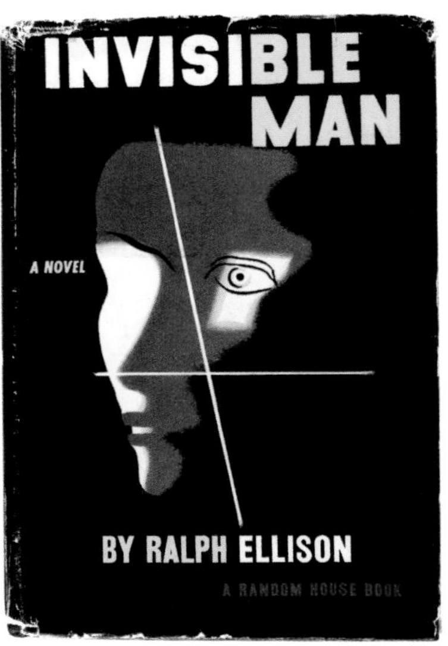
INVISIBLE MAN
A NOVEL
BY RALPH ELLISON
A RANDOM HOUSE BOOK

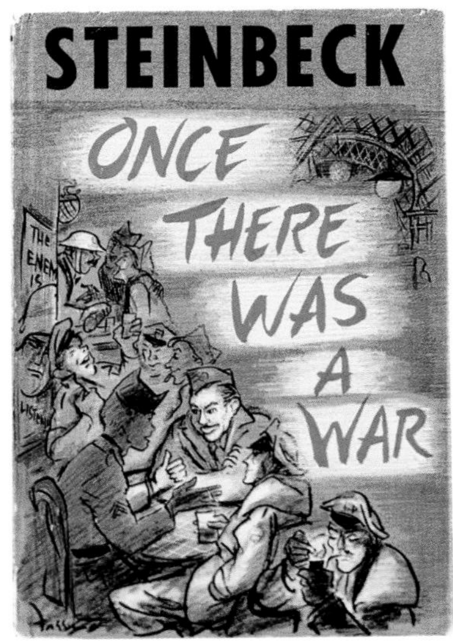
STEINBECK
ONCE THERE WAS A WAR

THE FAVORITE PHOTO

Among Marilyn Monroe's personal belongings were dozens of prints of this portrait taken by Cecil Beaton on February 22, 1956, in New York. She confessed it had always been her favorite, and she often included an autographed copy when she wrote back to her fans.

Joshua Logan, the director of *Bus Stop*, gave Marilyn the photograph in an engraved triptych, flanked by two handwritten pages by Cecil Beaton recalling this shoot. Beaton saw her as a very paradoxical figure, a siren and tightrope-walker, femme fatale and naive child, the last incarnation of an eighteenth-century face in a portrait by Greuze living in the very contemporary world of nylons, sodas, jukeboxes, and drive-ins.

What really struck Cecil Beaton was Marilyn's ability to keep transforming herself, to give the photographer a thousand variations of herself, without inhibition but with a real uncertainty and vulnerability—even though her incandescent beauty gave her the paradoxical freedom not to fuss over her clothes and her hair.

This photograph is just such an improvisation. Marilyn pulled this carnation from a bouquet to put in her mouth like a cigarette, only later lying on a sofa to place the flower on her breast in a gesture of protection and gift.

"She has rocketed from obscurity to become our post-war sex symbol, the pin-up girl of an age," Beaton wrote. "And whatever press agentry or manufactured illusion may have lit the fuse, it is her own weird genius that has sustained her flight. Transfigured by the garish marvel of Technicolor cinemascope, she walks like an undulating basilisk, scorching everything in her path but the rosemary bushes." He concluded, "Perhaps she was born just the post-war day we had need of her. Certainly she has no knowledge of the past. Like Giraudoux's Ondine, she is only fifteen years old, and she will never die."

Ambassador Hotel, New York, 1956

FUNERAL EULOGY

by

Lee Strasberg

Marilyn Monroe was a legend.

In her own lifetime she created a myth of what a poor girl from a deprived background could attain. For the entire world she became a symbol of the eternal feminine.

But I have no words to describe the myth and the legend. I did not know this Marilyn Monroe.

We, gathered here today, knew only Marilyn—a warm human being, impulsive and shy, sensitive and in fear of rejection, yet ever avid for life and reaching out for fulfillment. I will not insult the privacy of your memory of her—a privacy she sought and treasured—by trying to describe her whom you knew to you who knew her. In our memories of her she remains alive, not only a shadow on a screen or a glamorous personality.

For us Marilyn was a devoted and loyal friend, a colleague constantly reaching for perfection. We shared her pain and difficulties and some of her joys. She was a member of our family. It is difficult to accept that her zest for life has been ended by this dreadful accident.

Despite the heights and brilliance she had attained on the screen, she was planning for the future: she was looking forward to participating in the many exciting things she planned. In her eyes and in mine her career was just beginning. The dream of her talent, which she had nurtured as a child, was not a mirage. When she first came to me I was amazed at the startling sensitivity which she possessed and which had remained fresh and undimmed, struggling to express itself despite the life to which she had been subjected. Others were as physically beautiful as she was, but there was obviously something more in her, something that people saw and recognized in her performances and with which they identified. She had a luminous quality—a combination of wistfulness, radiance, yearning—to set her apart and yet make everyone wish to be part of it, to share in the childish naivete which was at once so shy and yet so vibrant.

This quality was even more evident when she was on the stage. I am truly sorry that the public who loved her did not have the opportunity to see her as we did, in many of the roles that foreshadowed what she would have become. Without a doubt she would have been one of the really great actresses of the stage.

Now it is all at an end. I hope that her death will stir sympathy and understanding for a sensitive artist and woman who brought joy and pleasure to the world.

I cannot say goodbye. Marilyn never liked goodbyes, but in the peculiar way she had of turning things around so that they faced reality—I will say au revoir. For the country to which she has gone, we must all someday visit.

August 9, 1962

CHRONOLOGY

June 1, 1926
Birth of Norma Jeane Mortenson in Los Angeles, third child of Gladys Pearl Baker, born Monroe, of unknown father. The baby was immediately placed in a foster home, first of all with the Bolenders and then with various other families. Sometimes Grace Goddard, one of her mother's friends, looked after her.

June 19, 1942
At only sixteen years old, Norma Jeane married Jim Dougherty, who was five years her senior.

1945
First meeting and first photo shoot with André de Dienes.

August 1946
First contract with Twentieth Century Fox. Ben Lyon persuaded her to change her name to Marilyn, after the musical star Marilyn Miller, and Monroe, which was her mother's maiden name.

June 1950
First screening of John Huston's *The Asphalt Jungle*. Marilyn received rave reviews in spite of her relatively small part.

March 13, 1952
The nude calendar scandal. Marilyn's career was jeopardized, but her confession, "I was hungry," drew public support.

1953
Henry Hathaway's *Niagara*, in which she had a dramatic role, was a big hit, as was *Gentlemen Prefer Blondes*, directed by Howard Hawks, which came out the same year.

October 1953
Marilyn met the photographer Milton H. Greene at a reception given in honor of Gene Kelly.

November 4, 1953
Premiere of *How to Marry a Millionaire*, a brilliantly successful comedy.

January 14, 1954
Marilyn married baseball superstar Joe DiMaggio.

February 1954
Marilyn entertained American troops engaged in the Korean War while on her way to Japan. She considered this one of the most important events in her life.

August 10, 1954
The filming of *The Seven Year Itch* began in New York. The famous scene with Marilyn standing over an air vent trying to hold down her billowing skirt was filmed on September 15 in front of a flabbergasted crowd and to DiMaggio's great displeasure.

October 5, 1954
Official separation from Joe DiMaggio.

November 1954
Supported the appearance of Ella Fitzgerald at the Mocambo club, where it was unusual for African Americans to be booked. Marilyn kept her promise of sitting at a front-row table every night.

Christmas 1954
Marilyn decided to leave Hollywood and move to New York, even though a magnificent dinner had just been given in her honor. She traveled under the name of Zelda Zonk, wearing a black wig and sunglasses.

December 31, 1954
Marilyn and Milton H. Greene founded their own production company, Marilyn Monroe Productions, Inc.

January 15, 1955
At a press conference for the new production company, Marilyn said that henceforth she wished to handpick her parts and included Grushenka in Dostoyevsky's *Brothers Karamazov* as an example. The press seized on this comment to hold her up to ridicule.

April 8, 1955
From Greene's house in Connecticut, Marilyn appeared on a popular morning TV talk show, *Person to Person,* hosted by Edward R. Murrow. More than fifty million people watched the program.

Spring of 1955
Living in New York, Marilyn studied at the Actors Studio as well as taking private classes with Lee Strasberg.

She had sessions with her psychoanalyst, Dr. Margaret Hohenberg, up to five times a week.

February 25 to June 2, 1956

Marilyn returned to live in Hollywood to work on *Bus Stop*, directed by Joshua Logan. The terms negotiated with Fox were much more advantageous after the enormous success of *The Seven Year Itch*.

June 29, 1956

Marilyn and Arthur Miller were married in a civil ceremony; the religious ceremony took place on July 1 after Marilyn's conversion to Judaism.

June 14 to November 6, 1956

Marilyn and her husband went to London for the filming of *The Prince and the Showgirl*, directed by and starring Laurence Olivier, and produced by Marilyn's company. The couple lived at Parkside House in Surrey.

Spring of 1957

Marilyn fired Milton H. Greene from her production company.
In May she went to Washington to support Arthur Miller during his House Un-American Activities Committee (HUAC) hearing.

August 4 to November 6, 1958

The filming of *Some Like It Hot*. Relations with Billy Wilder and actors Jack Lemmon (cast despite competition from her friend Frank Sinatra) and Tony Curtis were tense. Marilyn regretted Wilder's choice of filming in black and white.

1960

The filming of *Let's Make Love*, directed by George Cukor, with Yves Montand (suggested by Arthur Miller after Gregory Peck, Cary Grant, Charlton Heston, and Rock Hudson had all withdrawn). Marilyn had an affair with the French actor.

March 8, 1960

Marilyn won the Golden Globe for best actress for her performance in *Some Like It Hot*.

July 18 to November 4, 1960

The filming of *The Misfits* in Nevada.

November 11, 1960

Press announcement of the separation of Marilyn and Arthur Miller.

February 7 to February 10, 1961

Against her will and following a "misunderstanding." Marilyn was forcibly admitted into Payne Whitney psychiatric unit in New York on the recommendation of her current analyst, Dr. Kris. Lee and Paula Strasberg, whom she called for help, couldn't legally intervene, as they were not family members. Only DiMaggio was able to effect her release. She then spent three weeks at Columbia Presbyterian Medical Center undergoing a rest cure.

November 19, 1961

Marilyn met John Kennedy at his brother-in-law Peter Lawford's Santa Monica house.

February 1962

Marilyn bought a house in Brentwood, a fashionable neighborhood in Los Angeles.

April 23, 1962

The filming of *Something's Got to Give,* directed by George Cukor and produced by Henry Weinstein, began. Because Marilyn was repeatedly late or absent, production stopped on June 8. The film was never finished.

May 19, 1962

President John Kennedy's birthday gala was held at Madison Square Garden in New York. Marilyn made a memorable appearance.

June 23, 1962

Marilyn began the long photo shoot for *Vogue* with Bert Stern that came to be known as "The Last Sitting."

August 3, 1962

Marilyn appeared on the cover of *Life* magazine.

August 5, 1962

Marilyn Monroe died at night at her house in Brentwood.

Karen Blixen (1885–1962)

On February 5, 1959, a luncheon was organized at Carson McCullers's house in Nyack, New York, with Karen Blixen, who, on a lecture tour of the United States, had expressed a desire to meet Marilyn Monroe. She wrote to the American writer Fleur Cowles Meyer on February 21, 1961: "I think Marilyn is bound to make an almost overwhelming impression on the people who meet her for the first time. It is not that she is pretty, but she radiates, at the same time, unbounded vitality and a kind of unbelievable innocence. I have met the same in a lion-cub, which my native servants in Africa brought me. I would not keep her, since I felt that it would in some way be wrong . . . I shall never forget the most overpowering feeling of unconquerable strength and sweetness which she conveyed. I had all the wild nature of Africa amicably gazing at me with mighty playfulness."

Truman Capote (1924–1984)

The author of *In Cold Blood* met Marilyn in 1950 on the set of John Huston's *The Asphalt Jungle*. They became close friends, and in *Music for Chameleons*, Capote dedicated a magnificent short story to her, entitled "A Beautiful Child."

Carson McCullers (1917–1967)

Carson McCullers met Marilyn through Arthur Miller in New York in 1954 and afterward saw her regularly. She described her memories of these meetings in her unfinished autobiography, *Illumination and Night Glare*.

Norman Mailer (1923–2007)

Norman Mailer lived in the same brownstone in Brooklyn as Arthur Miller and had a house not far from Marilyn and Arthur's in Roxbury, but despite his many sollicitations, he never met Marilyn. After her death, Mailer devoted two biographical essays to her, the first, *Marilyn*, in 1973, and the second, *Of Women and Their Elegance*, in 1980.

Somerset Maugham (1874–1965)

Maugham wrote to Marilyn to express his delight at the news that she was to play the part of Sadie Thompson in an adaptation of his short story "Rain," which Lee Strasberg hoped to direct for NBC, but the movie was never made.

Arthur Miller (1915–2005)

Marilyn met her future husband, along with Elia Kazan, in Hollywood in 1952. She was photographed by Ben Ross that same year, reading a book by Miller. When she moved to New York, he helped her move toward a more intellectual and cultured way of life. In spite of the disapproval of both the studios and her own circle, Marilyn courageously stood by Miller's side during his House Un-American Activities Committee hearing. Marilyn also met Saul Bellow through Arthur Miller.

Pier Paolo Pasolini (1922–1975)

He never met Marilyn Monroe, but a year after her death in 1963, he wrote an elegy to her, which was recited as a voice-over during a montage sequence in his film *La Rabbia*, with Albinoni's Adagio in G Minor as background music. He wrote, "You, little sister, had that beauty humbly bestowed on you, and your soul born from modest people never knew how to own it, for it would not be beauty otherwise. The world first taught it to you, and so took your beauty as its own."

Carl Sandburg (1878–1967)

Marilyn and the American poet met on the film set of *Some Like It Hot* in 1959. She was a great fan of his biography of Abraham Lincoln. They communicated mostly by phone, but there are photos of their joyous meeting at Irena and Henry Weinstein's home in January 1962. He wrote about her, "She was not the usual movie idol. There was something democratic about her. She was the type who would join in and wash up the supper dishes even if you didn't ask her."

Edith Sitwell (1887–1964)

Edith Sitwell and Marilyn Monroe first met and had tea together at the end of 1954, in Hollywood. Marilyn, with her golden hair and green dress, reminded the eccentric English poet of a daffodil. They got on well and discussed poetry, in particular *The Course of Life* by Rudolph Steiner. They met again in London in 1956.

Dylan Thomas (1914–1953)

When the Welsh poet was on a reading tour of the United States in February 1950, he expressed the wish to meet Charlie Chaplin; however, before his dinner engagement he had a great time drinking martinis with Shelley Winters and Marilyn Monroe. He arrived dead drunk at Chaplin's home and was turned away by the great comedian himself.

ACKNOWLEDGMENTS

Thanks to:

Sarah Churchwell

Ségolène Dargnies

Marion Duvert

Abby Haywood

Courtney Hodell

Karen Hope

Mark Krotov

Annie Ohayon

Flore Roumens

Ivana Ruzak

Lisa Silverman

Special thanks to Maja Hoffmann, who organized the dinner at the FIAC, and to Lou Reed, who was there.

PHOTOGRAPH CREDITS

page vi: © André de Dienes
page 3: © André de Dienes
page 4: © Silver Screen Collection/Hulton Archive/Getty Images
page 12: © Christie's Images/The Bridgeman Art Library/Jock Caroll
page 13: Archive photo
page 30: © André de Dienes
page 31: © Eve Arnold/Magnum Photos
page 48: © mptvimages.com
page 49: © Joshua Logan/private collection
page 86: © Michael Ochs Archives/Getty Images
page 87: © Rue des Archives/SPPS
page 102: © André de Dienes
page 103: © Elliott Erwitt/Magnum Photos
page 104 (top): © Bob Haswell/Getty Images
page 104 (bottom): © Roger Viollet/Ullstein Bild
page 122: © Dave Cicero
page 123: © 2010 Mimi Ross, photograph by Ben Ross
page 132: © André de Dienes
page 133: © George Barris
page 146: © Bettmann/Corbis
page 147: © Bettmann/Corbis
page 174: © Michael Ochs Archives/Getty Images
page 192: Private collection
pages 198–99: Private collection
page 206: © André de Dienes
page 214: © George Silk/Life Magazine/Time & Life Pictures/Getty Images
page 215: © Arnold Newman/Getty Images
page 226 (top, middle left, middle right): © Christie's Images/The Bridgeman Art Library, private collection
page 226 (bottom): © Shaan Kokin/Julien's Auctions
page 227: © Christie's Images/The Bridgeman Art Library, private collection
page 229: © Cecil Beaton/Camera Press/Rapho-Gamma
page 230: © Peter Basch